Video Game Programming for Kids

Jonathan S. Harbour

Course Technology PTR

A part of Cengage Learning

COURSE TECHNOLOGY
CENGAGE Learning·

Australia • Brazil • Japan • Korea • Mexico • Singapore • Spain • United Kingdom • United States

Video Game Programming for Kids
Jonathan S. Harbour

Publisher and General Manager,
Course Technology PTR:
Stacy L. Hiquet

Associate Director of Marketing:
Sarah Panella

Manager of Editorial Services:
Heather Talbot

Senior Marketing Manager:
Mark Hughes

Senior Acquisitions Editor:
Emi Smith

Project Editor:
Jenny Davidson

Technical Reviewers:
Jeremiah Harbour and
Kayleigh Harbour

Interior Layout:
Jill Flores

Cover Designer:
Mike Tanamachi

Indexer:
Sharon Shock

Proofreader:
Sara Gullion

For product information and technology assistance, contact us at
Cengage Learning Customer & Sales Support, 1-800-354-9706
For permission to use material from this text or product,
submit all requests online at **cengage.com/permissions**
Further permissions questions can be emailed to
permissionrequest@cengage.com

All trademarks are the property of their respective owners.

Library of Congress Control Number: 2012930790

ISBN-13: 978-1-4354-6116-1

ISBN-10: 1-4354-6116-9

Course Technology, a part of Cengage Learning
20 Channel Center Street
Boston, MA 02210
USA

Cengage Learning is a leading provider of customized learning solutions with office locations around the globe, including Singapore, the United Kingdom, Australia, Mexico, Brazil, and Japan. Locate your local office at: **international.cengage.com/region**

Cengage Learning products are represented in Canada by Nelson Education, Ltd. For your lifelong learning solutions, visit **courseptr.com**
Visit our corporate Web site at **cengage.com**

Printed by RR Donnelley. Crawfordsville, IN. 1st Ptg. 03/2012
Printed in the United States of America
1 2 3 4 5 6 7 14 13 12

To Jeremiah, Kayleigh, Kaitlyn, and Kourtney.

Acknowledgments

Thanks to Emi Smith and Stacy Hiquet for seeing the potential for this book! Thanks to Jenny Davidson for her wonderful editorial work. Thanks to Jeremiah and Kayleigh for their many days of hard work previewing the book to make sure it was good for kids. Thanks to Galleon for creating and releasing QB64 for free.

About the Author

Jonathan S. Harbour is a freelance writer and game developer. He maintains a forum at http://www.jharbour.com/forum for support of his books and games, and he has a Facebook page at http://www.facebook.com/jharbourcom. He enjoys science fiction, comics, and video games.

Contents

Introduction

This book will teach you how to write your own video games using the BASIC language. You will learn all the basics of programming from the very beginning. *No experience required!*

The programs in this book will work with a free BASIC compiler called QB64 (see the link below in the Downloads section). QB64 is a modern variation of QuickBasic that supports all previous versions of BASIC dating back to the 1960s (including programs with or without line numbers and programs with subs/functions). You can load nearly any old .bas or .qb file into QB64 and it will run!

This book teaches structured programming at a very easy level, so the reader will learn good programming techniques without getting stuck in complexity. The writing style of this book was kept intentionally simple, as the target age group is 8-12 (although a gifted youngster or an older teen may still enjoy it).

Most examples in this book do not require any extra files, as the example games are self contained. The exceptions are the last two chapters, which use bitmaps and sounds. The reasoning behind this approach is to enable a child (our target reader) to type in a program and have it run without any problems. For a learner who is new to programming, missing bitmap and sounds files can lead to frustration. At this early level, we avoid that problem by having the programs themselves create images with BASIC graphics commands.

The last two chapters are for the more advanced reader. It is recommended that a parent or teacher copy the files as described to get the last two example games to run. Any files you wish to load into a game should be copied into C:\QB64. See the links below in the Downloads section.

To ensure that the programs in this book work properly, and that the chapters are fun and readable, two child reviewers previewed the text, tested the games, and commented on each chapter.

This is more than just a book "For Kids"; it is an homage to the past. Any programmer today who started with BASIC in "the old days" may find this a fun read. I got my start in programming with a book called *IBM PC Graphics* by John Clark Craig. I also used to read magazines like *Compute!* that featured BASIC programs you could type in. It is in homage to these that this book was written. Many books and tutorials today assume too much: too much complexity and too many expectations! It is my sincere hope that you enjoy this book as much as I enjoyed BASIC long ago when I was just a beginner.

Mahalo,

Jon Harbour

February 25, 2012

Downloads

You can download QB64 from **http://www.qb64.net**. QB64 does not need to be installed so it will run from anywhere! I recommend installing it to C:\QB64 since that is the folder referenced in the book.

All of the programs in **Chapters 1-10** can be typed in and run without any extra files. If you want to load the programs into QB64 instead of typing them in, the source code for all of the examples in this book can be downloaded directly from here:

http://www.jharbour.com/book resources/1169-resources.zip

The files are all in one big folder (which is how it was done in the old days with BASIC). Just copy all of the files into C:\QB64 for easy access. QB64 was designed to be copied as needed, not "installed." It is easier to use if you store your programs in this folder with it.

The book resources are also available on the publisher's website at http://www.courseptr.com/downloads (search by book title or author). Please note that you will be redirected to the Cengage Learning site.

The author's website also features a discussion forum where the files for this and other books can be downloaded:

http://www.jharbour.com/forum

Chapters 11-12

There are three files needed for the AlienBeetles.bas game, and two more files for the BitmapDemo.bas program in Chapter 11. You can type these locations into a web browser to download the files. Save these files to C:\QB64. (*These files are also included in the zip file. If you have any problems downloading these files, just download the complete resource zip file.*)

* http://www.jharbour.com/book resources/beetle.png
* http://www.jharbour.com/book resources/bullet.png
* http://www.jharbour.com/book resources/ship_side.png
* http://www.jharbour.com/book resources/ship_white.png
* http://www.jharbour.com/book resources/ship.png

There are also just three files needed for the "Bomb Catcher" game in Chapter 12. (Save these files in the C:\QB64 folder.)

* http://www.jharbour.com/book resources/bomb.png
* http://www.jharbour.com/book resources/basket.png
* http://www.jharbour.com/book resources/explode.wav

Tutorials for Parents/Teachers

There are a *few* QB64 lessons available for parents and teachers (lessons, assignments, quizzes). These materials *do not* correspond one-for-one to the chapters in the book. If you would like to use these materials, visit the author's forum and look in the BASIC section. These are *not* official instructor materials, just bonus teaching aids created by the author and not supported by the publisher. In addition to the files, the lessons are posted online: see the author's free "Game Programming Primer" course at http://www.udemy.com/game-programming-primer.

Styles

The layout for the "For Kids" series was designed with ease of readability as the primary goal. The text layout is simple with a large font, narrow paragraphs, and short source code listings. One callout style is used for important points to remember: Secret.

 This is a special feature of the book that offers helpful advice and other secrets to the reader!

Chapter 1

Hello, Stinky Head

Have you ever wondered how games like *Super Mario Kart Wii* or *Battlefield 3* or *Call of Duty: Modern Warfare 3* are made? Maybe you have played a lot of games and wondered how they do it? Well, the truth is, you *can* make your very own video games with the help of this book. They won't be as awesome as the big fancy games just mentioned, because games like those cost millions of dollars and take hundreds of people to make!

They're *big budget* games, and it takes a lot of work, like making a movie. But, it is possible to make your own *simpler* video games. That is how most of the pros who work for big companies like Electronic Arts get started, by reading books like this and learning all they can until they grow up and get a job! You can do that some day if you really want to and work hard at it.

To make a video game, you will learn *programming*. This means that you write a program and the computer runs it. In the old days when computers were relatively new, only experts knew how to write computer programs. These experts are still needed today, working for places like NASA and IBM and Microsoft on complex robots and things.

Computer scientists are people who do experiments by writing programs to see what will happen. But computers are much easier to program than they used to be. Almost anyone can do it with a little bit of help. You can do it too!

BASIC

You are going to learn how to program with a compiler called QB64. So, what is that?

QB64 is not the name of a robot like C3PO, but I think it's a great name for a robot! QB64 is a program that lets you do programming. Yes, you have to use a program to write your own program! In the old days, computer experts made computers out of wires and vacuum tubes (sort of like a light bulb used for memory). These computers were really "dumb" back in the old days. But give them a break; even computers start off like babies and need to grow!

QB64 is what you will use to make video games in this book. The "QB" part stands for "Quick Basic." The "64" part just sounds fancy but doesn't mean anything. It's not even a 64-bit program, but it supports 64-bit computers, so I guess it's okay.

Quick Basic is an old programming language that Microsoft invented to make programming a little easier for beginners. It started off as a language just called BASIC, which was invented in the 1960s.

BASIC stands for this:

B   Beginner's

A   All-purpose

S   Symbolic

I   Instruction

C   Code

BASIC is a programming language. By learning the language, you will be able to write programs that tell the computer to do something.

You can even boss it around if you want! You can tell the computer nice things, or you can be mean, and it won't mind. Computers are very patient and don't get upset.

Some day, very soon, there will be robots like C3PO for real, that you can talk to, and that will walk around and do things. Won't that be great? If you love robots, then you can learn how to program now, and then you'll be ready to maybe get into robot programming. Ask your parents or teacher about LEGO MINDSTORMS (http://mindstorms.lego.com). LEGOs won't be as great as C3PO, because robots are still new technology too, but soon...very soon... they'll grow up.

Baby Computers

Baby computers (meaning old-school computers) did not know how to run programs; they had to be programmed with wires and memory tubes the hard way. Sometimes it took close to three days to wire up the computer to be a calculator, just to do addition and subtraction problems. Some of the first computers were invented by the army to help them fire artillery guns. Today, the army has missiles that can think on their own, fly around with a *camera* for eyes, and fly around things while looking for a target! It's a shame something so smart just blows up when it hits the enemy!

Computers are a lot smarter today. They were invented in the 1940s during World War II, which was only about 70 years ago. That sounds like a long time when you're a kid, but just think, there are people alive today who remember the world before computers! Can you imagine spending a whole week or maybe a whole day without ever using your computer?

Did you know that cars have computers in them? Yep, I'm serious. Every new car made today is run by a computer. The car can't even run without the computer. So, if the computer breaks, the car won't run. Can you believe it? Sometimes when a car breaks down, a programmer has to fix it instead of a mechanic. That's so weird. Some police cars today even have a phaser beam like weapon that can shut down a bad guy's car's computer if he is trying to escape! (So, the trick is to drive an old getaway car! Shh, don't tell anyone I said that!)

Getting QB64

You might need to ask a parent or teacher to help you get QB64. It has to be installed on your computer. You can download it from a few different places:

* From the website at www.qb64.net.
* From the book's web page at www.courseptr.com/downloads.
* From the author's website at www.jharbour.com/forum.

When you download QB64, it will come in a zip file. Save the files inside the zip onto your computer. There is no installer for QB64. All you do is download the zip file, copy the files out of it onto your computer, and then it's ready to run.

There are a whole bunch of files and folders inside the QB64 zip file. Some of them are pretty cool to learn about, like jpeg.dll. This file lets QB64 load photos. You can use a photo in a video game if you want. Some programmers use JPEG files for the graphics in their video game. I prefer to use a different picture file called PNG ("ping"); it is also supported thanks to the help of libpng12-0.dll. There are other files, like libogg-0.dll and lib-vorbis-0.dll, which support music files for video games. I love video games with awesome music. There's another file called smpeg.dll that adds support for movie files! So, you see, all the weird files that come with QB64 really have important jobs to do. As a programmer, you need to learn things like this. This is uber-secretive information, so don't tell "regular" users these things. Only programmers are allowed.

The most important file of them all is qb64.exe. That's the big daddy—the one you want to run in order to use QB64! If you want to stop someone from using QB64, you could rename this file to something like qb64- hahaha.exe. Then they won't be able to find it anymore. But, that would be rude, right? (Technically, I'm supposed to tell you "don't do that.")

Ask your parent or teacher to create a shortcut to qb64.exe on the Windows desktop, unless you already know how to do it yourself. A shortcut makes it easier to run the program, since QB64 doesn't get "installed"; you just run it. No installer. Zip. Nada. I kind of like that.

Running QB64

When you run QB64, it looks like this (see Figure 1.1):

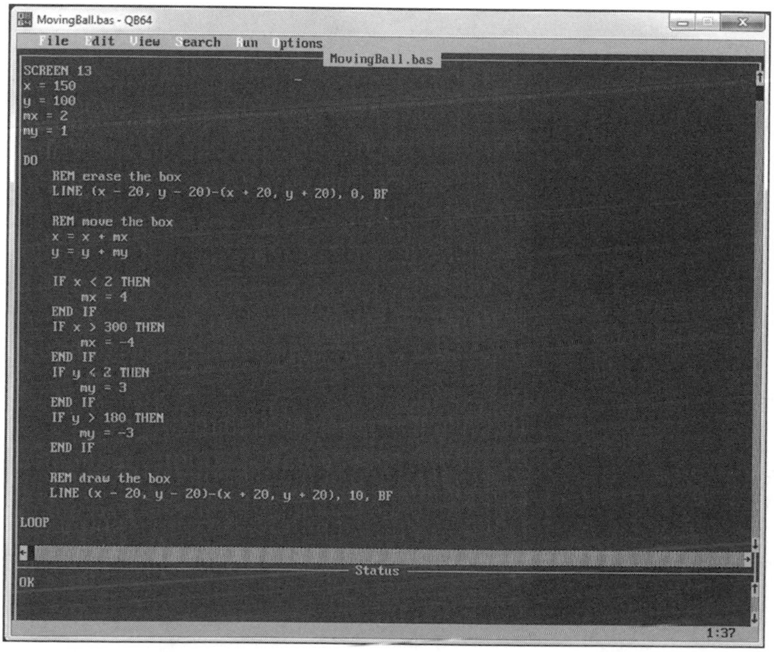

Figure 1.1

This is QB64 with a program already typed in.

When you run QB64 for the first time, it will just come up with a blank blue screen. This is the editor. An editor means you can edit your program. Editing means typing. When you type in the editor, you are programming! You could just type "ABCDEFG" and presto, you're a programmer! That program might not *do anything*, but you're still a programmer.

 It's kind of a pain to say QB64 over and over again, so let's just say BASIC from now on. QB64 = BASIC. I hope you don't mind. If you don't like it, then just pretend I'm saying QB64 each time you read BASIC.

Programmers write programs. The programs are typed into an editor. Then, after typing the program, you have to save it to a file. The typing you do writes a program. Writing programs is called *coding*. Writing "code." We also call that "programming," so they mean the same thing. When you write a program, you're writing *source code*, and you are a *coder*! Both words mean the same thing, but I like to say *programmer* more often. Let's do that now; write some *code*.

"Hello, Stinky Head!"

Type in this program:

```
PRINT "Hello, Stinky Head!"
```

That's all.

Yes, there's only the one line!

Now, you wrote your first line of code, and have become a programmer cadet. You have a long way to go to become a captain, let alone a general! But we aren't in the army, and there aren't any ranks for programmers. Well, there are, sort of. Let's just make up our own, shall we?

If you are a beginner, then you're a Youngling. It's a "nice" way of saying that you aren't great at programming. But don't worry, you'll learn fast.

If you know enough to write a short program and run it, then your skill level is like a Padawan Learner. The keyboard is like your light saber. Hey, be careful with that thing! You just know enough to be dangerous.

If you are skilled enough to write a video game, then you are a Master! A Master can easily make a video game without needing to look in the book for help.

You have much to learn before you will be a Master, but I am sure you'll make it by the last chapter, if you study hard and pay close attention!

That one line program prints out a message. Run it by using the Run menu in BASIC (remember, that means QB64 from now on). The menu is shown in Figure 1.2. In the Run menu, choose Start. Or, you can press the F5 key to run the program without using the menu.

Your program has to be *perfect* in order to work. If you make even one little mistake, BASIC might not run your program. It isn't very smart! Even the littlest mistake will keep the program from running! Just be careful to type in the program exactly as it is shown, with all the quotes and commas in the right places.

It will take a couple seconds for the program to start up. At the bottom of BASIC, it will say, "Creating EXE file...". Then, a black window will come up with a message in it. (See Figure 1.3.)

Now, change the message that gets printed out. Change it to anything you want. Just make sure there are quotation marks around the message. A quotation mark (") tells BASIC that this is going to be a message to print out.

Programmers call the message a *text string* or just *string*.

Figure 1.2

Using the Run menu to run the program.

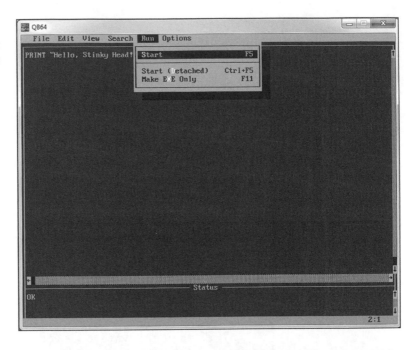

Figure 1.3

The program prints out the message "Hello, Stinky Head!" in the window.

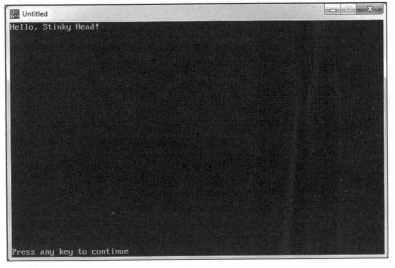

That's a strange word for a message: *string*. It's not the kind of string you can use to tie up bad guys, or climb up the side of a building, or to climb out of a tree. But, that's just what it's called, and it's a silly name. In programming, sometimes things don't make sense.

Some funny words are used to mean things in programming that don't mean the same thing in English. Some Masters like to play jokes on us.

That isn't the computer's fault; it's the names invented by people, not computers. People make up some funny names for computer programs. There's one called Java, which is a kind of coffee. What's next, hot chocolate? The fancy word for hot chocolate is *mocha*, so I wouldn't be surprised one bit to find a language called Mocha. If I were inventing my own programming language, I would maybe call it Cylon, which means Cybernetic Lifeform Node. Then, when I meet the guy who invented Java, I could say, "Oh yeah, well I invented Cylon. I'll bet you don't know it!"

Let's go back to the program. Did you get your own message—oops, I mean, *string*—to print out in the window? After changing—I mean, *editing*—the program by replacing "Hello, Stinky Head!" with your own string, does it run? Press F5 to watch it run again after changing the string. Did it work? If you forget the quotation marks, then BASIC might complain!

Here's an example (see Figure 1.4). I typed in my own string, replacing the original one, and left out the quotation marks. Look what happened! BASIC refused to run the program! It says at the bottom, "Expected operator in equation on line 1". That's just a fancy way of saying there's an error in line 1. BASIC even changes the color of the line to red for you. This is like a red alert in the source code. This is a pretty smart editor.

Have you ever wondered why the compiler doesn't just fix the errors for you? If it's smart enough to see the errors, why can't it just change them real quick?

That's a great question. The reason the compiler can't change the errors is because the compiler is not a programmer, and it isn't allowed to change the programmer's code. The nerve!

This error happened because there are no quotation marks around the string. But if I change it—I mean *edit* it—by adding the quotation marks back in, then it will run like it should. As soon as you fix the error, then the red color goes away, the message at the bottom goes away, and BASIC seems to be happy again. Just look at it now after I fixed the errors (see Figure 1.5):

Figure 1.4

BASIC won't even run a program with errors in it.

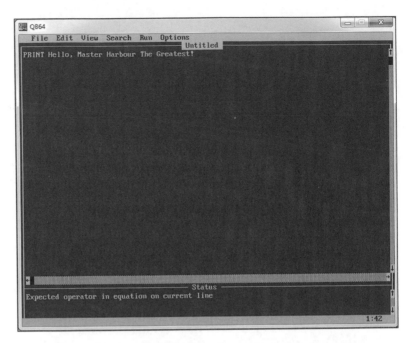

Figure 1.5

When there are no errors in the program, BASIC just says "OK" at the bottom.

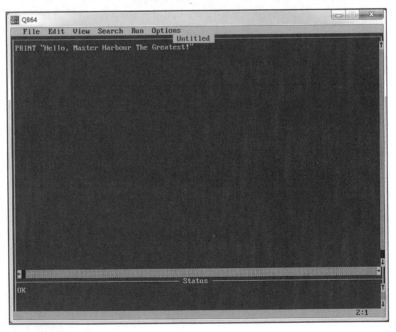

Let's Do Some Serious Programming: Variables

Are you ready for more? I am! We just covered the basics of using BASIC (QB64), just to make sure it works. In programming, the most important thing to learn about first is how to use *variables*.

A *variable* is a small piece of memory in the computer that you can name whatever you want. You could name it *A* or *HaHaHa* or *wowthisisreallyridiculous91827364555*. The only thing is, you can't start a variable with a number, like *1B* or *123lookatme*. Variables have to start with a letter.

There are two main types of variables, depending on whether they are numbers or strings (remember that word, string, means a message).

A *number variable* is a variable that holds a number. For example, *age* might be a variable that holds a number.

A *string variable* is a variable that holds a string. String variables have a special symbol at the end that makes them special: the dollar sign ($). When BASIC sees the dollar sign ($) at the end of a variable, it knows this is a string.

Oh, brother, why is it a dollar sign? I have often asked myself the same question. I think some clever programmer thought it looked like an S (for string). I can't help but think of money when I see a dollar sign. But, as a programmer, you will get used to it. It's just one of those funny things in programming that we have to learn. (In other words, how to put up with goofy things people do.)

An example of a string variable is *name$*.

When you want the variable to hold memory, then use the equal sign to fill it with some number or string. In programming, the equal sign is used to set a variable equal to something. That *something* is called *data*. Data is information. For example:

```
age = 10
```

This creates a variable called age, and sets it to a value of 10. You can use any number you want, like:

```
age = 75
```

or

```
age = 81450
```

Okay, that isn't a very realistic age, so maybe it's the age of dinosaur bones, not the age of a person.

A string variable might be:

```
name$ = "Elliot"
```

Here are some more examples:

```
name$ = "Sarah, Queen of Egypt"
name$ = "John, Spartan 117, UNSC"
name$ = "Inigo Montoya"
```

Each time the variable, name$, is changed, the old string is replaced with the new one. The names aren't all added together when you use the equal sign to set the variable. But, we *can* add strings together, as a matter of fact!

```
name$ = "Bobby " + "Fisher"
```

When name$ is printed out, then it will show "Bobby Fisher".

There are more ways you can work with the plus sign. For instance:

```
firstname$ = "Qui-Gon"
lastname$ = "Jinn"
wholename$ = firstname$ + lastname$
```

Here, we are using three separate string variables for the name, and this works just fine. You might be wondering why in the world anyone would do it like that. That's a good question. It's just an example of what BASIC can do. As a programmer, you will have to figure out creative ways to solve programming problems that come up while making your video games. Knowing all the features of BASIC is very helpful.

A Master knows all the tricks. You can't learn *all* of the tricks by just reading about them; some tricks can only be learned by programming.

Getting User Input

A computer program—including a video game—must do three things, and always only three things. We'll call them the three rules of programming:

1. Get input.
2. Think about it.
3. Print output.

Even a video game works by following these three important rules. The thing is, a video game doesn't have to *print* with a string or message. That item #3 can be changed to mean "Draw output." The important thing is, something comes out of the program. In a video game, we will want to draw shapes, like players, monsters, trees, houses, and things like that.

Can you think of what the input for a video game might be for step #1?

I'll let you think about it for a minute....

Ready with your answer?

Okay, I'm sure you got it right, but just to check, the answer is: input from a keyboard, mouse, or a controller.

Here's another question for you: What is the best video game system: Xbox 360, PlayStation 3, or Wii?

The correct answer is Xbox 360. Did you get it right?

You can get user input from the computer's keyboard or mouse always. But if you want to program a video game for the Xbox 360 (or one of the other less awesome systems), you would have to use a special compiler. Normally, normal humans aren't allowed. Only humans with red hair and purple eyes are allowed to program a PlayStation 3. For the Nintendo Wii, only humans with giant round eyes are allowed. If you don't look like that, then you have to hire someone who does to get the compilers for you, and then you can use it. Once you trick Sony or Nintendo into giving them to you, by hiring people who look like that, then you can make games for those systems.

But, they let *any person* program an Xbox 360! See why it's so great? You don't even have to look weird. Once you become a Master, you will have the knowledge to program games for Xbox 360.

Oh, I'm so just kidding, of course. What I meant was, it's so hard to get permission to program PlayStation 3 or Wii that it *seems* like that to me. That part is true. But, you can program video games on the Xbox 360 without getting special permission.

 When you become at least a Padawan if not a Master, then you can read the book *XNA Game Studio 4.0 for Xbox 360 Developers* to learn how to program video games on the Xbox 360.

Where were we? Oh yes, back to getting user input. You can use INPUT to let the user type something into BASIC. Here's a program you can try out:

```
INPUT "What is your name: ", name$
PRINT "Hello, "; name$
```

Now go ahead and run the program. Remember how? I'll give you a hint: It's in the Run menu. When you run it, the program looks like Figure 1.6.

Figure 1.6

Getting INPUT *from the user.*

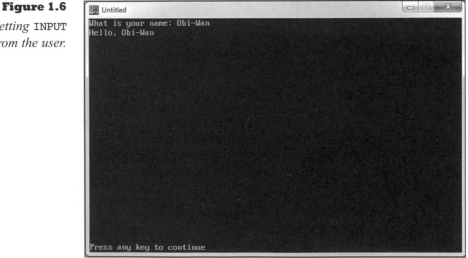

This little program lets you type in your name and then it prints out a greeting in return! This program follows two of the three requirements of a functional program. Do you remember the three rules? Here they are again:

1. Get input.
2. Think about it.
3. Print output.

Can you tell me which of these steps that last program did?

First, we did #1 by using INPUT.

Next, we did #3 by using PRINT.

What's missing is #2, thinking about it. How do we make BASIC think about something? Ah, I'm glad you asked. Let's learn how to do that.

Thinking...

In BASIC, you can make the computer think. That's right, think! It's really great when you learn how to do this, because then you will be writing really useful programs that meet all three rules. To help BASIC think about something, we use a special word called IF.

People use IF all the time, but you aren't even aware that you're doing it, because you've been thinking your whole life. But, if you think about it for a minute, when you're making decisions, you're asking yourself questions. For instance:

```
IF I eat this cookie before dinner, Mom will get upset.
```

Isn't that thinking?

Here's another one:

```
IF you get three strikes, then you're out!
```

There are also more complex decisions we have to make every day, such as:

```
IF I choose a hamburger,
    THEN I won't get a hot dog.
```

What about making decisions with two results?

```
IF my bike's tire is flat,
    THEN I have to walk to school.
    OTHERWISE, I'll get to ride my bike.
```

Let's use IF to make a program that can think. I'll use the cookie example first. Here's the program you can type in:

```
INPUT "Did you eat the cookie (yes/no)? ", answer$
IF answer$ = "yes" THEN
    PRINT "Oh, no, you are busted!"
END IF
IF answer$ = "no" THEN
    PRINT "Good answer."
END IF
```

Go ahead and run the program. When the question comes up, be sure to type yes or no in lowercase like it says. If you type any word besides yes or no, then nothing gets printed out. This is kind of dumb, but that's how the program works.

Another helpful word we can use is ELSE. This one lets you have more than one answer, depending on the question. In programming, we call this logic. All "thinking" is called logic. IF is a logic statement in BASIC. The programming term for IF is a *conditional statement*.

Here's a new version of the program that uses ELSE to make it better. You can just *edit* the program. You don't have to start over.

```
INPUT "Did you eat the cookie (yes/no)? ", answer$
IF answer$ = "yes" THEN
    PRINT "Oh, no, you are busted!"
ELSE
    PRINT "Good answer."
END IF
```

There's one thing about ELSE you have to know: It takes care of any other word you type in besides yes (in this program). So, if you type "blargh" or "brainz" it will still print out the same thing, "Good answer.". That's okay, because all we really care about is when the user types yes. If he types yes, then he gets busted!

Now that you learned how to make BASIC think, can you write your own fun program that thinks about different things?

Write your own thinking program using IF on any subject you want. For instance, you could make a trivia game that asks the user a bunch of questions. Oh boy, that sounds like fun. There's just one problem—we need to keep track of score. How do you do that?

The Trivia Game

We're going to make a trivia game using IF to make the program think about our answers. You can add your own questions to the bottom of the program if you want by just following the example. To keep track of score, we have to learn to do some math in BASIC.

A number variable called score is used in the Trivia Game. Start off by setting score = 0. Then, when you want to add a point to the player, you add 1 like this:

```
score = score + 1
```

This looks kind of strange, but what it means is, add one to the current score, and then save that new answer in the score variable again.

Here is the complete source code for the Trivia Game. When you type it in, go ahead and run it once to make sure the game works, then start adding your own questions. The last question, #4, is blank, so you can use that for starters. Then copy that exact same code for question #5.

```
score = 0
PRINT "Welcome to the Trivia Game"
PRINT

PRINT "QUESTION 1"
INPUT "Are you the greatest programmer in the world?",
answer$
IF answer$ = "yes" THEN
    PRINT "Correct!"
    score = score + 1
ELSE
    PRINT "Wrong! It's yes."
END IF
PRINT "SCORE: "; score
PRINT
```

```
PRINT "QUESTION 2"
INPUT "What is Obi-Wan's last name? ", answer$
IF answer$ = "Kenobi" THEN
    PRINT "Correct!"
    score = score + 1
ELSE
    PRINT "Wrong! It's Kenobi."
END IF
PRINT "SCORE: "; score
PRINT


PRINT "QUESTION 3"
INPUT "Who was Nemo's friend, the purple fish?", answer$
IF answer$ = "Dory" THEN
    PRINT "Correct!"
    score = score + 1
ELSE
    PRINT "Wrong! It's Dory."
END IF
PRINT "SCORE: "; score
PRINT

PRINT "QUESTION x"
INPUT "<add your own question>", answer$
IF answer$ = "<edit>" THEN
    PRINT "Correct!"
    score = score + 1
ELSE
    PRINT "Wrong!"
END IF
PRINT "SCORE: "; score
PRINT

PRINT "GAME OVER"
```

The Trivia Game was intended for you to edit with your own questions. Just use this example for starters. When it's run, the program looks like Figure 1.7:

Figure 1.7

Playing the Trivia Game.

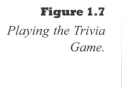

```
Untitled
Welcome to the Trivia Game

QUESTION 1
Are you the greatest programmer in the world?yes
Correct!
SCORE:  1

QUESTION 2
What is Obi-Wan's last name? Vader
Wrong! It's Kenobi.
SCORE:  1

QUESTION 3
Who was Nemo's friend, the purple fish?Simba
Wrong! It's Dory.
SCORE:  1

QUESTION x
<add your own question>
Wrong!
SCORE:  1

GAME OVER

Press any key to continue
```

Summary

That's the end of the chapter. No more will I teach you today. Clear your mind of questions… good… good. Remember, a programmer's strength *flows* from the code. For starters, you learned how to print strings, how to get input, how to use variables, and how to make the program *think*. That is a really great start.

Quiz

Here is a little quiz to test whether you were paying attention or not. Try to answer the questions without looking up the answers first. This is not graded; it will just tell you whether you are ready to go to Chapter 2 or not. The answers are found in Appendix A.

1. What BASIC command prints out words on the screen?

A. HELLOB. PRINT

B. PRINT

C. INTEGER

D. IF

2. What program do we use to write BASIC programs?

A. Visual Basic

B. QBASIC

C. QB64

D. BASIC-A

3. Which one of these is a good string variable?

A. name$ = "Master Chief"

B. name = 100

C. $name = The Arbiter

D. name$ = Grunt

4. Which one of these is a good number variable?

A. number = "7"

B. number$ = 8

C. number = '4'

D. number = 5

5. What BASIC statement lets the program think?

A. IF...THEN...ELSE

B. THINK

C. IF...END

D. THINK...STOP

Homework

Your homework for this chapter is required to really prove that you understand what you learned. If you have a hard time with this homework, then maybe you went too fast and might need to review the chapter again.

Instructions:

The Trivia Game comes with three sample questions and one fill-in question at the end. Change the questions and answers and make *your own* trivia game. You could also make a quiz about any subject you want and then have your friends take the quiz to see how smart they are. You can cover any subject you want, but the game or quiz must have 10 questions, and it must keep score. The winner is the person who gets the most questions right.

Chapter 2

You Forgot Your
Combination?!

Video games have a lot of math in them. If you're good at math, then it's a little easier to program more advanced video games. But even if math isn't your best subject, you can learn the math tricks programmers use in their video games. It's just about learning something new. Like any subject, sometimes you have to work a little harder to learn it. But, when you learn it, you know it and then it's easy. I'm not talking about the math to launch a spaceship to Mars or something! What I mean is, we can start off with easy problems and learn how to make a simple game with random numbers.

The Guessing Game

You're going to make a classic game called the Guessing Game. The computer will think of a number from 1 to 100, and you have to guess what it is. You will have to use a bunch of new BASIC commands that you haven't learned about yet. But that's okay; this is all part of the learning experience! For example, you are just learning basic programming with words. Soon, you will be doing graphics. Since graphics is a harder subject, you have to learn about programming with PRINT and INPUT first. Let's get some more practice right now! Type in the following program and run it to make sure it works. It should look like Figure 2.1 if you've typed it in correctly. Good luck!

SECRET

If you see REM at the start of a line, that means that line is a comment. Comments are like notes that help explain what the programmer intended, so others can understand it. You can also use a single quote (') for comments. These are valid comments:

```
REM This is a comment
' This is also a comment
```

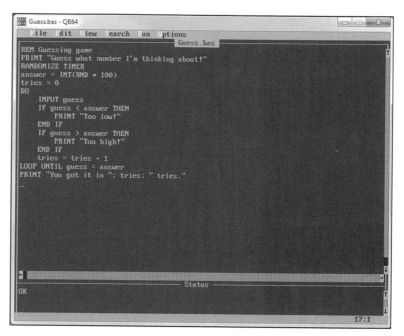

```
REM Guessing game
PRINT "Guess what number I'm thinking about!"
RANDOMIZE TIMER
answer = INT(RND * 100)
tries = 0
DO
    INPUT guess
    IF guess < answer THEN
        PRINT "Too low!"
    END IF
    IF guess > answer THEN
        PRINT "Too high!"
    END IF
    tries = tries + 1
LOOP UNTIL guess = answer
PRINT "You got it in "; tries; " tries."
```

When you run the program it will look like the next screen (Figure
2.2). I got the answer in 7 tries. Can you get a better score?
Sometimes the computer thinks of a really hard number that takes
longer, and sometimes you get lucky with an easy one (like 50). I
got it one time in only 4 guesses, because the computer thought of
the number 1 and I started off by guessing 12 the first time, and it
said "Too high!" So, I guessed lower and got it really fast that way.
But, since there's no picture, I can't prove it! So, see if you can get
the answer in less than 7 guesses to beat my score.

Figure 2.2

The Guessing Game program is running.

```
Untitled                                                    _  □  x
Guess what number I'm thinking about!
? 12
Too low!
? 20
Too low!
? 90
Too high!
? 80
Too high!
? 50
Too high!
? 40
Too low!
? 45
You got it in  7  tries.




Press any key to continue
```

SECRET
Remember to Save your program before closing QB64 or starting a new program. You may want to open the program again later and run it without typing in the code from scratch.

This is a pretty fun game. If you want, you can change the words to insult the players when they get the answer wrong (just for fun). Like, if they take more than 10 tries to get the answer, then they really stink at it! Or, you can add a line to encourage the player if he does well. Here's an example. Try adding this line to the very end of the program after the last line.

```
IF tries < 5 THEN PRINT "Wow, you are amazing!"
```

Did you notice anything different about this thinking line (starting with an IF)?

Well, I don't know if you noticed this or not, but the PRINT is on the same line as the IF...THEN. In the past, we always had to put the PRINT part on a new line, and then include an END IF and that took three lines. Now, this one is only on one line. Why?

If you just need to do one little thing, you can put it at the end of the IF line, like I did with this example. But if you want to do more than one thing, like, printing and adding to the score, then you have to do it the longer way with END IF at the bottom.

Here's another fun thing you can add to the game at the very end:

```
IF tries > 10 THEN PRINT "You stink at this game!"
```

You can use IF...THEN to make your program "think" in order to solve problems.

I want to explain the program to you. Look at the next picture (Figure 2.3). First, the program starts making random numbers with RANDOMIZE TIMER. This is a neat feature. This shuffles the random number generator, so the computer thinks of a totally different number every time you run the program. Normally, the computer will produce the same random numbers over and over again when you run the program. This special command makes sure that doesn't happen (which would be dumb, as the game would be too easy).

Next, the computer thinks of a number from 1 to 100. This is the part where RND is used. RND creates a random number—that means the computer thinks of a different number each time.

Random means a number that you can't predict will come up. It makes the computer act trickier. Programmers *love* RND. It helps make monsters and things harder to beat.

You can follow along from here, as each step is explained in the picture.

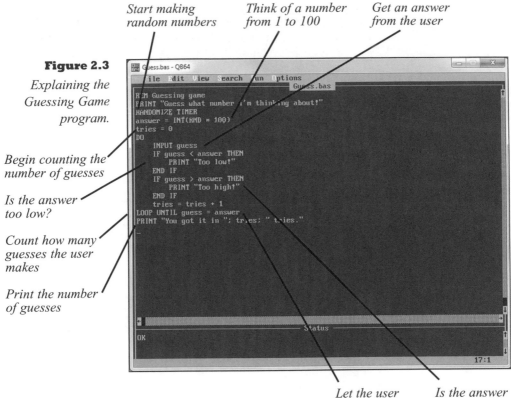

Start making random numbers

Think of a number from 1 to 100

Get an answer from the user

Figure 2.3

Explaining the Guessing Game program.

Begin counting the number of guesses

Is the answer too low?

Count how many guesses the user makes

Print the number of guesses

Let the user guess again!

Is the answer too high?

The Rude Computer

Let's make a new game that uses random numbers again. We can use RND to have the computer choose a random sentence whenever you type something in, and it will be like you are talking to the computer, and it is talking back. You can change the things that the computer says by just writing different sentences instead of the ones shown. Every DATA line is a comment that the computer will make after you type something. So, go ahead and run it and then try changing the sentences to say whatever you want. If you want to add more replies, you can add more DATA lines, but just be sure to change the num = 8 to how many lines there are in total (if you add 2 more lines, then set num = 10, for example).

The RESTORE command tells BASIC to start reading DATA lines again from the very beginning after it has read them already. The READ command reads the next line in order.

```
PRINT "I Am The Rude Computer"
INPUT "What is your name? ", name$
PRINT name$; " is a dumb name."
RANDOMIZE TIMER
num = 8

DATA "You are a super dunder head."
DATA "Well, I don't care about that."
DATA "Oh really? You are so wrong."
DATA "Can I talk to a smart person, please?"
DATA "I think you are special. Not!"
DATA "How dare you speak to me in that tone!"
DATA "How does that make you feel?"
DATA "I'm not sure what to say."

DO
    INPUT ">> ", user$
    n = INT(RND * num)
    RESTORE
    FOR n = 1 TO n
        READ answer$
    NEXT
    PRINT answer$
LOOP UNTIL user$ = "quit"
PRINT "Fine, be that way."
```

All done typing it in? Okay, run the program by pressing F5. I saved the program in a file called RudeComputer.bas, which is included in this chapter's files on the www.courseptr.com/downloads site. If you don't want to type in the program you can load this file into BASIC and just run it. But, it's better to type it in yourself, to improve your skill as a programmer. Once you've finished and tested that the program works, it should look like this (see Figure 2.4).

Now, how about making some changes to the program? That's the best way to learn—by changing a program with your own new ideas. How about converting it into a program called The Polite Computer, and have it say only nice things? Go ahead, try it! All you have to do is change the sentence in each DATA line to what you want it to say.

Figure 2.4

*I Am The Rude
Computer.*

```
Untitled                                                    _ □ X
I Am The Rude Computer
What is your name? Steve
Steve is a dumb name.
>> no it's not!
I think you are special. Not!
>> you aren't either
You are a super dunder head.
>> no you are!
How does that make you feel?
>> I feel like you are a dork
How does that make you feel?
>> i just told you dummy
Oh really? You are so wrong.
>> no i'm not you are
How dare you speak to me in that tone!
>> oh really?
How does that make you feel?
>> quit
How dare you speak to me in that tone!
Fine, be that way.



Press any key to continue
```

SECRET

Some computer experts work on trying to make computers smarter. That field is called artificial intelligence. You know, robots like WALL-E and C3PO and R2D2 are really just computers with bodies.

The way this program works is, the computer thinks of a random number from 1 to 8, and then prints out one of the 8 sentences in the DATA lines based on that number. Sometimes it even seems like you're really talking to the computer. The program works this way by using DO...LOOP. These two commands work together to repeat the same lines in BASIC over and over again. If you add an option after the LOOP then you can make the loop stop.

Like this, for example:

```
LOOP UNTIL user$ = "quit"
```

That line waits until you type quit when talking to the computer. When the program sees that user$ = "quit", then the loop ends. The computer gets one last rude comment in before the program ends:

```
PRINT "Fine, be that way."
```

Loops are very important in programming. They let us program things to repeat as many times as we want them to. You could have a loop repeat 3 times, or 100 times, or a million times, and BASIC will just do it. It's cinchy compared to writing a million lines yourself. That's what computers are really great at doing—repeating things over and over again really fast. Humans aren't that good at it. But there's something we can do way better than any computer: We're better at thinking about problems, and doing art, and playing music.

Robots Love Their States

The next thing you're going to learn about is keeping track of more than one thing at a time in a program. Computer experts call it *finite state programming*. Good grief, isn't that a complicated name? No, it's easy. Like many things in life, this only *looks* hard, but when you look carefully it's not. The word "finite" means limited, which means small. Do you know what the opposite of that is? *Infinite* is the opposite! That means unlimited, which means large. Really, infinite means it has no end; it goes on forever. Since we can't even imagine forever, we can just say "really huge" to get the point.

By "really huge," I'm thinking of, like, the whole galaxy, not just something large like an elephant or an Apatosaurus (like the one shown in Figure 2.5). That's a huge animal, but the size of a galaxy is so huge it's hard to imagine. In comparison, a dinosaur is just a few times larger than an elephant, but what about a whole galaxy?

Figure 2.5

Drawing of an Apatosaurus. Image courtesy of Wikipedia Commons.

Here is a drawing of the Milky Way galaxy (see Figure 2.6), with a big bright center where there is a super-massive black hole (billions of times more powerful than the Sun). The galaxy spins around that black hole at the center, creating the spiral-shaped arms. Those spirals contain 300 *billion* stars. Our Solar System and Earth are just one of those stars. But that's not the half of this grand story! Nearby our galaxy are *other* galaxies. Together, they are all part of a *cluster*. Then, there are even larger groups of clusters called super clusters. And there are *millions* of super clusters in the universe as far as telescopes can see. Now *that's* what I'm talking about—that's huge. But, as incredible as it sounds, the whole universe is like a grain of sand on a beach compared to infinity.

Figure 2.6

Drawing of the Milky Way galaxy. Image courtesy of Wikipedia Commons.

Now, where were we? Oh, that's right, we were learning about *finite state*. The next word is *state*. That just means, what you're doing at the moment. You might be riding your bicycle, or playing a video game, or getting ready to go to school. These are things you might be doing—or your *state* at one minute during the day. Put the two words together, and we get *finite* and *state*, which means, a small number of things you might be doing. This is a basic idea in computer science that is used in many programs.

NASA builds and sends robots to Mars on rockets to explore the planet. These robots use *state* when they are rolling around on Mars, taking pictures, smelling the dirt, and doing other funny things. Here is a picture of NASA's three Mars robots (see Figure 2.7). The dinky one in the middle was called the Sojourner mission; the one sent to Mars is called *Pathfinder* (it is about the size of an R/C car). The bigger robot on the left was called the Mars Exploration Rover mission, and two of them were sent to Mars: *Spirit* and *Opportunity* (they are about the size of a quad). The *biggest* robot on the right is called the Mars Science Laboratory mission and it is about the size of a car! Right now *Curiosity* is on a space ship heading toward Mars, and will get there in 2012.

Figure 2.7

NASA's Mars robots. Image courtesy of Wikipedia Commons.

These awesome robots, or *rovers* as NASA calls them, run by *state programming*. Can you think of some states that a robot on the surface of another planet like Mars might go through?

I can think of one: When the sun goes down and it becomes night-time, the rover goes to sleep because it is solar powered and the battery won't last long without sunlight to power it up.

Here's another state: When NASA asks the rover to send a photo, the rover goes into photo state, where it takes a photo and then sends it back to Earth in something like an e-mail. Wouldn't it be great to get an e-mail from *Curiosity*? If that were the case, then it would be in *e-mail state*. Here's what it might say:

```
From: Curiosity/MARS
Date: 12/04/2012 3:33 PM (Earth Time)
To: jsharbour@gmail.com
Dear Jonathan,
I'm sorry you're stuck back there on Earth, because I'm
exploring another planet and it's awesome. If you were
here, you would have to wear a spacesuit because there's
hardly any air to breathe. The ground is crunchy and
sandy when my wheels roll over it, like a desert. By the
way, you are wrong about my power system. I don't have
solar panels like Spirit and Opportunity; I have a
radioisotope thermoelectric generator (RTG). I don't need
to shut down at night and dust storms don't slow me down.
Well, I have to go do more important things now, so have
a nice sol (that's what you call a day on Mars).
Your friend,
Curiosity
P.S. Did you know one day on Mars lasts 24 hours and 39
minutes?
```

You can change the state of something by just giving it a certain number. So, let's say, when you're eating breakfast, your state = 1. When you're playing outside, your state = 2. When you're cleaning your room, your state = 3. So, if I wanted to force you to clean your room forever, I could just set you to 3, and never change it! Ha, ha!

You Forgot Your Combination?!

Let's make a game called Combination Lock to learn more about states. In this game, you have to guess the combination of three numbers in the right order to open the lock and get the treasure (let's pretend the treasure is a brand new copy of *Legend of Zelda: Skyward Sword*, autographed by Link!). The source code for the game is coming up next. There is a DO...LOOP section that asks the user to type in three numbers, and then it looks at those numbers to see which ones are right. When you get one of the combination numbers wrong, it tells you which direction to turn the combination (higher or lower) next time you type them in. Pretend that you're turning the dial on a safe; that's kind of what is happening in this game.

The RANDOMIZE command is important, because without it the computer would choose the *same* combination every time you run the program!

```
PRINT "Combination Lock Game"
PRINT "Guess the combination lock if you can!"
PRINT "Each number will be from 1 to 6."
RANDOMIZE TIMER
guesses = 0
state = 1

REM make the combination lock
number1 = INT(RND * 6) + 1
number2 = INT(RND * 6) + 1
number3 = INT(RND * 6) + 1

DO
    correct = 0
    INPUT "Guess #1: ", num1
    INPUT "Guess #2: ", num2
    INPUT "Guess #3: ", num3

    REM check #1
    IF num1 = number1 THEN
        correct = correct + 1
        PRINT "#1 is correct!"
    ELSE
        IF number1 > num1 THEN PRINT "#1 is higher"
        IF number1 < num1 THEN PRINT "#1 is lower"
    END IF


    REM check #2
    IF num2 = number2 THEN
        correct = correct + 1
        PRINT "#2 is correct!"
    ELSE
        IF number2 > num2 THEN PRINT "#2 is higher"
        IF number2 < num2 THEN PRINT "#2 is lower"
    END IF

    REM check #3
    IF num3 = number3 THEN
        correct = correct + 1
        PRINT "#3 is correct!"
```

```
        ELSE
            IF number3 > num3 THEN PRINT "#3 is higher"
            IF number3 < num3 THEN PRINT "#3 is lower"
        END IF

        guesses = guesses + 1
LOOP UNTIL correct = 3

REM the player wins
PRINT "You opened the lock and got the treasure!"
PRINT "It took you "; guesses; " guesses."
```

After typing the game into BASIC, it should look something like Figure 2.8.

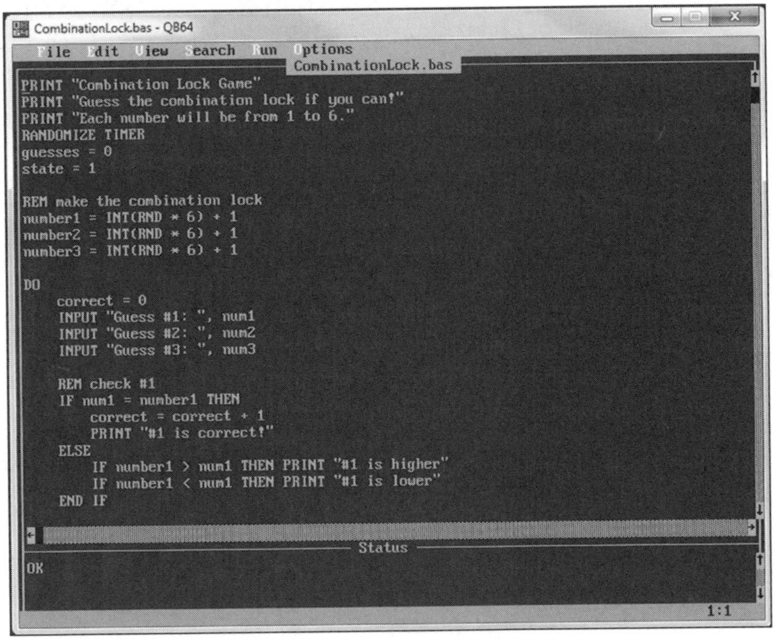

Figure 2.8

The Combination Lock game source code in QB64.

When you run the game, it will ask you to type in three numbers at a time, and then it will print out the results of each number. If you got the right number, it will tell you that you got it right. If any number is wrong, it will tell you that the correct number is either higher or lower than the one you tried. You can use these clues to narrow down the right combination to the lock! In the screen shown in Figure 2.9, I got the answer in four tries—I got lucky, as two numbers were right on my first try. See if you can beat my score!

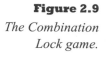

Figure 2.9

The Combination Lock game.

```
Untitled
#1 is correct!
#2 is higher
#3 is correct!
Guess #1: 3
Guess #2: 4
Guess #3: 3
#1 is correct!
#2 is higher
#3 is correct!
Guess #1: 3
Guess #2: 5
Guess #3: 3
#1 is correct!
#2 is higher
#3 is correct!
Guess #1: 3
Guess #2: 6
Guess #3: 3
#1 is correct!
#2 is correct!
#3 is correct!
You opened the lock and got the treasure!
It took you  4  guesses.

Press any key to continue
```

Dungeon Master

Some of the oldest computer games were called Text Adventures, or TADs for short. These were games where you would type in commands and then read about what happens after each turn. A TAD game is programmed using state programming too, like the last program. We're a bit out of time now for a large example TAD, but we can see a small one to at least give you some ideas about how to make this kind of game. Here is the source code for the game that you can type in:

```
100 PRINT "What is your name: ";
200 INPUT name$
300 PRINT "Welcome to the dungeon, " + name$ + "!"
400 PRINT "What is your command: ";
500 INPUT c$
600 IF c$ = "attack" THEN 700
650 PRINT "You ran away."
660 GOTO 800
700 PRINT "You destroyed the monster!"
800 END
```

This game does not have a DO...LOOP section, which means it only asks you one time and then replies to your command before ending. This isn't much of a game because you can only do one thing. But, can you figure out what that one thing is, and type it into the game when it runs? I'll give you a hint: If you type anything other than "attack," you will just run away like a chicken—like I did in this instance (see Figure 2.10).

Figure 2.10

I ran away like a chicken.

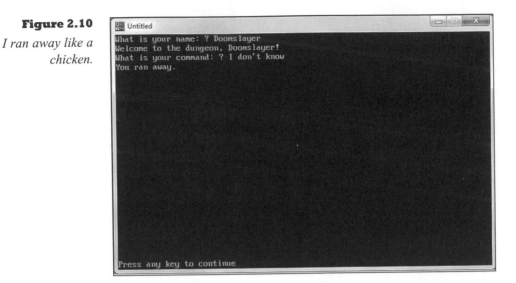

Did you notice something weird about this short game? It has line numbers in front of every line! While the plot of the game is questionable (I don't even remember seeing anything about a monster until it gets slain!), the purpose of this little gem is to show you what old BASIC programs used to look like. Way, way, way back in the old days, BASIC programs had line numbers like this. Today, we write programs without line numbers using IF...THEN...END IF and DO...LOOP, but in the early years of BASIC you would have to use GOTO to jump to a line number.

Summary

Congratulations on finishing this chapter! You learned a lot of really great new things about programming in BASIC—some very helpful and important things! Now, see if you can get all the quiz questions right and try the homework assignment to see how well you understand the things you learned.

Quiz

Here is a little quiz to test whether you were paying attention or not. Try to answer the questions without looking up the answers first. This is not graded; it will just tell you whether you are ready to go to the next chapter or not. The answers are found in Appendix A.

1. What BASIC statement is used for a remark or comment line (for making notes)?

A. REM

B. IF

C. COM

D. NOTE

2. Which command generates a random number (like rolling dice)?

A. INT

B. TIMER

C. RND

D. STR$

3. What does RANDOMIZE do?

A. It creates a random number.

B. It shuffles the random number generator.

C. It simulates rolling dice.

D. It is like a phaser weapon.

4. What statement starts a loop?

A. DON'T

B. LOOP

C. START

D. DO

5. What statement ends a loop?

A. DO

B. FOR

C. LOOP

D. END

Homework

Your homework for this chapter is required to prove that you understand what you learned! If you have a hard time with this homework, then maybe you went too fast and might need to review the chapter again.

Instructions:

The Dungeon Master game is pretty neat, but it can be very hard to write a program with line numbers, as you shall see, bold adventurer! See if you can modify the game so that it understands one more command. It already knows what to do if you type in "attack". Add a new command called "defend" that prints out a different message before ending. Be careful not to mess up the code already there, since it works! You might also want to print a message at the beginning that tells the explorer about the monster and gives them some instructions.

Chapter 3

Save the Hangman

Now that you can do some BASIC programming, we can learn more about one of my favorite subjects—graphics! Sometimes, graphics programming means just drawing one pixel or dot at a time. To make a whole picture, like the scene of a game, you *could* draw it with dots and other shapes, like circles and squares. If you want your game to look really awesome, a better way is to load a bitmap and draw it all at once—but we'll hold off on bitmaps for a while yet. Learning about graphics is really fun if we take it in stages and just start programming. So, we'll look at all of the graphics statements and commands in QB64 in this chapter.

Changing the Screen

In the old days, back in the 1970s and 1980s, computers had very low quality screens. Back then, a computer screen was called a monitor, or a CRT—Cathode Ray Tube. It looked like an old-fashioned TV, because, well, it was! There were some personal computers back then that did not come with a monitor at all; instead, you would plug it into your TV like you do with a video game system—like your Xbox 360, Nintendo Wii, or Sony PS3, to name the newest consoles at this time. We can take for granted the crazy high-resolution LCD monitors today because they are so affordable, but this would have been unbelievable technology back then. Widescreen was unheard of at that time!

Today, your typical PC has a 20" or larger widescreen LCD—Liquid Crystal Display. There is even a newer technology coming out now for TVs and computer monitors: LED—Light Emitting Diode. An LED screen is made up of millions of little LEDs, just like the blinking lights on a phone or the power light on a radio. The LED used for a power indicator is usually red or green. Well, an LED screen uses the same technology but the diodes are tiny, crammed onto the flat screen, and for every pixel there is one little tiny red, green, and blue diode.

Red, Green, and Blue—RGB: these are the three main colors used in computer graphics. They are the prime colors that rule all other colors. By using Red, Green, and Blue, in different combinations, you can create *any other color*! Including black (0, 0, 0) and white (255, 255, 255).

What are those numbers in parentheses? That is how you define an RGB color, in that order: (Red, Green, Blue).

The range for the numbers goes from 0 to 255. Yes, sometimes you want one of them to be 0, so the other one or two prime colors get more attention. That's very important!

For instance, here is the RGB code for.... Well, wait a minute, how about if *you* do it? Do you know what two colors make *Yellow*?

I'm sure you know that, because it's pretty easy: Red and Green. The code for Yellow is (255,255,0). Notice in this code that Blue is 0. That causes there to be *no blue* at all in the color. If blue tint is added, it will darken the yellow.

Let's play with some colors in BASIC.

Open up QB64 if you don't have it open already. Are you ready to go? Okay, make sure it's a new program, just blank. Now, type in these two lines and press F5 to run it.

```
SCREEN _NEWIMAGE(800, 600, 32)
CLS 2, _RGB(255, 255, 0)
```

SECRET   800 × 600 is an old resolution dating back to the early 1990s. It was called "Super VGA" or SVGA. The important thing about it is the ratio of the width and height, which is 4:3. You say "4:3" as "four to three."

It means for every four points to the right, go three points down. If you multiply 4:3 by 10, you get 40:30. Multiply it by 100 and you get 400:300. By 200, you get 800:600. You don't *have* to use a 4:3 ratio for your games, but it's a standard.

Widescreen is usually 16:9 ("sixteen by nine"). If you have an HDTV in your living room, the resolution is 1920 × 1080. That's where we get *1080p*.

When it runs, a big window should appear with a bright yellow background, as you can see in Figure 3.1.

SCREEN is a new command. This is the first graphics command in BASIC that you need to use to support graphics mode. In BASIC, the normal mode is text mode. You used text mode before to print messages and let the user type in words. In graphics mode, you can draw all kinds of shapes.

Figure 3.1

Clearing the screen with yellow.

Let's look at that SCREEN statement again.

```
SCREEN _NEWIMAGE(800, 600, 32)
```

This code instructs BASIC to make a window with a resolution of 800 × 600. That's a pretty good window size, but you can try different sizes to find one you prefer to use. But, be sure your window size will run on someone's computer if they have an older monitor. 1200 × 1000 is the highest I would go up to if I were you.

Statements and *commands* mean the same thing. You can use either word to describe the sub-procedures and functions in BASIC. Technically, a statement is a bit more than that, but the words are used interchangeably.

Pausing at the End

Did you notice the words at the bottom: "Press any key to continue"? We didn't program that! BASIC is just trying to be helpful. You see, if you don't do anything to cause the program to wait, it will just pop up and then close again really quickly. BASIC is being helpful by making the program wait so you can see it. This is normal. But when we're doing graphics, that message doesn't work.

So, let's get rid of the helpful message by making the program wait on our terms. Add these new lines to the program to cause it to wait for the user to press a key. This way, the window will look nice and clean, and the program will still pause before closing. The new lines are in bold.

```
SCREEN _NEWIMAGE(800, 600, 32)
CLS 2, _RGB(255, 255, 0)
DO
LOOP UNTIL INKEY$ = CHR$(27)
SYSTEM
```

When you run the program with F5, it comes up without the message at the bottom. The screen just shows a yellow background. So, that works, but what does the DO...LOOP do?

You have seen DO...LOOP before, but as a reminder, it causes some code to be repeated. In this case, you want it to repeat until something weird happens with INKEY$. So, what is INKEY$?

INKEY$ gets the character code for a single key press. Every key on the keyboard has its own character code. The code is called ASCII—American Standard Code for Information Interchange. ASCII goes way back! It's how information is sent on networks between computers. For example, when you open up your favorite website, your computer is talking to another computer (the web server). That web server sends your computer a web page using ASCII. All this means is ASCII is text. Like the words in this book.

For example, Space is ASCII code 32.

In the little program you just wrote, the loop keeps running UNTIL INKEY$ = CHR$(27). Can you figure out what that means? I'm sure you can now that you know how to read BASIC code.

INKEY$ does *nothing* if you aren't pressing any key. But, if you do press a key, then INKEY$ sends back the ASCII code of that key. The way you can check for a certain key is by using a helper statement called CHR$.

```
LOOP UNTIL INKEY$ = CHR$(27)
```

CHR$ returns the "character" of an ASCII code. Code 27 is the Escape key!

There's another way you can use INKEY$—by just telling it what key you want to look for in quotes. Like, the B key, for example:

```
LOOP UNTIL INKEY$ = "B"
```

Go ahead and run the program with this change. What happens? Does the program end when you hit the B key on the keyboard?

No?

You might be surprised by this, but INKEY$ knows the difference between lowercase and uppercase letters. If you want to get this program to work, press Shift+B. There—it should close now.

If you want to make the program close with just the lowercase "b" key, then change it to look like this:

```
LOOP UNTIL INKEY$ = "b"
```

Getting Key Codes

So, if you can just type in the letter you want to use in a game, why do we need CHR$ at all? That's a good question! The answer is: because some keys don't have a letter! Like the Escape key. There's no printable character that goes with the Escape key, only ASCII code 27. Some other keys are like that. Can you spot them on your keyboard? The function keys (F1, F2, F3, etc.), the arrow keys (Up, Down, etc.), Page Up, Page Down, Home, End, and so on. There are a lot of these types of keys! So, what we learned is that INKEY$ doesn't really look at keys; it looks at the code for a key.

What do you suppose is the code for the Up arrow key?

I have a better idea: you could write a program that prints out the code when you press a key. Why do something the hard way when your computer can do it for you?

```
DO
    k$ = INKEY$
    IF k$ <> "" THEN
        code = ASC(k$)
        PRINT k$; " = "; code
    END IF
LOOP UNTIL k$ = CHR$(27)
SYSTEM
```

The program works pretty well for getting the code of a normal key, but as you can see in Figure 3.2, there's a problem with some of the keys printing out a 0.

Figure 3.2

Printing the ASCII code of any key.

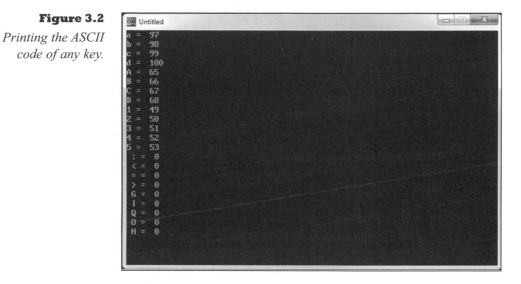

This isn't an error. INKEY$ returns a special code when you press one of the extended keys, like Up, Home, F1, F2, Insert, etc. To take care of that problem, INKEY$ will return *two codes* for the extended keys. The trick is figuring out how to get the second code.

Here is a new version of the program that shows how to do it. When a special key is pressed, the code returned by INKEY$ is 0. When that happens, we use the ASC statement to get the second byte.

```
PRINT "Key Decoder Program"
DO
    k$ = INKEY$
    IF k$ <> "" THEN
        code = ASC(k$)
        IF code = 0 THEN
            code = ASC(k$, 2)
        END IF
        PRINT k$; " = "; code
    END IF
LOOP UNTIL code = 27
SYSTEM
```

The program is shown in Figure 3.3. See how the special keys come out looking weird? The ASCII code for the Up arrow is 72, but it printed out as an " H" (space in front). The space comes from the 0 code, and the "H" comes from the 72 code. 72 is really the ASCII code for H, but the PRINT statement doesn't know we're doing something special here.

Figure 3.3

Printing the special codes for extended keyboard keys.

Wouldn't it be great if we could look up just the name of the key and not have to do all this hard work to use special keys?

Yes, of course, that would be helpful, because we need to use those special keys in most of our games. The arrow keys are used a lot in games. The W-A-S-D keys are also used often, especially in shooters and RPGs (Role-Playing Games) where you control a character in the game.

Do you think you could improve the program so it prints out the names of the extended keys? I'll just give you one to help get you started. The semicolon at the end makes the word "Up" print on the same line as the ASCII code printout.

```
IF code = 0 THEN
    code = ASC(k$, 2)
    IF code = 72 THEN PRINT "Up";
END IF
```

Clearing the Screen

We got a little off track learning about keys because that was also important, but now we can get back into graphics again. Let's review the first program again:

```
SCREEN _NEWIMAGE(800, 600, 32)
CLS 2, _RGB(255, 255, 0)
```

You already learned about the SCREEN statement.

The second line in this program clears the screen using the CLS statement. There are two *parameters*. A parameter is an option. Some parameters are required; some are not. It depends on the statement.

The first parameter is 2, which tells CLS to clear the screen in graphics mode.

The second parameter is the background color.

In the old days, this would just be a number from 0 to 15. That still works, but we want to use more complex colors. The _RGB statement is a helper. You just give it three prime color values to create a new custom color! (255, 255, 0) is yellow, of course.

```
CLS 2, _RGB(255, 255, 0)
```

Drawing Circles

The CIRCLE statement draws a circle. There are three parameters or options:

```
CIRCLE (X, Y), Radius, Color
```

The location parameter is made up of X and Y parts like this: (X, Y). This is where the circle will be drawn from its *center*. Remember that the location is the center of where you want the circle to be in the window.

When you're using 800 × 600 mode, the X values go left to right, starting at 0 on the left, and going to the right to 799; meanwhile, the Y values go up to down, from 0 to 599. It may be confusing to start counting at 0 instead of 1, but that's how you do it in computer graphics.

The illustration in Figure 3.4 shows what these parameters mean when drawing a circle.

Figure 3.4

Illustration of a
CIRCLE.

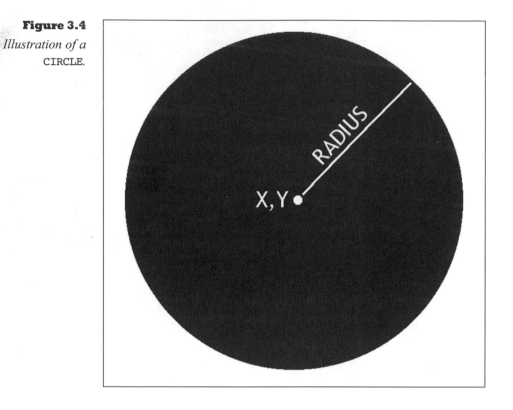

Let's draw one big circle that takes up the whole window. Here's an example program that draws a circle.

```
SCREEN _NEWIMAGE(800, 600, 32)
DO
    CLS 2, _RGB(0, 0, 80)
    CIRCLE (400, 300), 250, _RGB(255, 255, 255)
LOOP UNTIL INKEY$ = CHR$(27)
SYSTEM
```

The running program is shown in Figure 3.5. There's just one problem with this program—it flickers. Badly! The flicker is caused by the CLS statement, which clears the window, and then the circle is drawn, and then erased again, very quickly.

There's just no way to draw the circle fast enough to stop it from flickering. The only way to stop the flickering is to change the way BASIC draws when doing graphics. The graphics system in QB64 redraws the screen automatically. That's a good clue toward solving the flicker problem.

Figure 3.5

Drawing a very large white circle.

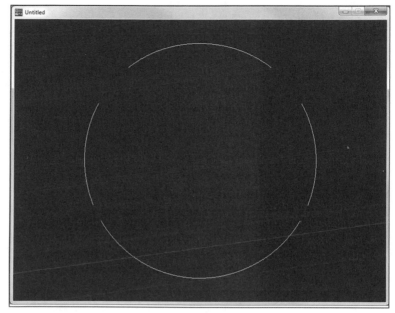

Here's a secret statement I'll show you how to use that will take care of it. The _DISPLAY statement tells QB64 (which does all the graphics in our BASIC programs) to wait until we're ready to redraw the screen. If you put _DISPLAY on a line after you're done drawing, then it will clear things up. Try it.

```
SCREEN _NEWIMAGE(800, 600, 32)
DO
    CLS 2, _RGB(0, 0, 80)
    CIRCLE (400, 300), 250, _RGB(255, 255, 255)
    _DISPLAY
LOOP UNTIL INKEY$ = CHR$(27)
SYSTEM
```

That's a handy statement! You'll have to remember to use it whenever there's a flickering problem.

Drawing Many Circles

If you want to draw a bunch of shapes, you would have to write one extra CIRCLE statement for every circle you want to draw. But there's an easier way to draw a lot of things: it's called looping.

FOR..NEXT is the most common type of loop. You have already used DO loop quite a bit, but that goes forever. A FOR loop runs only a certain number of times, and then it quits.

In BASIC, a FOR loop looks like this:

```
FOR n = 1 to 10
   PRINT "n = "; n
NEXT
```

Everything inside the FOR and NEXT lines is repeated 10 times, as you can see in Figure 3.6.

```
FOR n = 1 to 10
   PRINT "n = "; n
NEXT
```

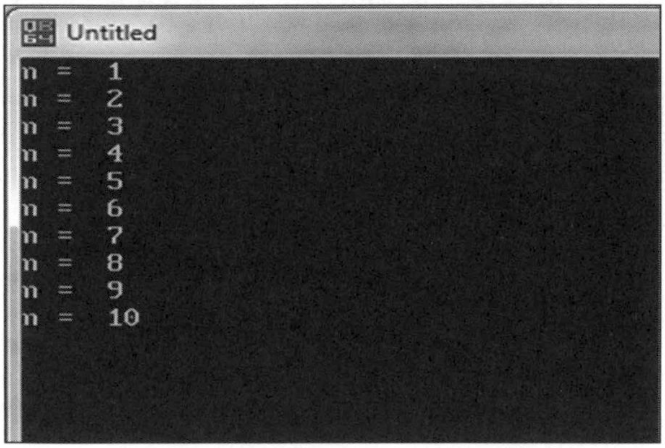

Figure 3.6

Printing numbers in a FOR *loop.*

Let's try a different loop range, like 1 to 100. This program loops 100 times:

```
FOR n = 1 to 100
   PRINT "n = "; n
NEXT
```

You can also count down *backwards* using the STEP statement! This program does that, and you can see what the program looks like when run in Figure 3.7.

```
FOR n = 20 to 1 STEP -1
   PRINT "n = "; n
NEXT
```

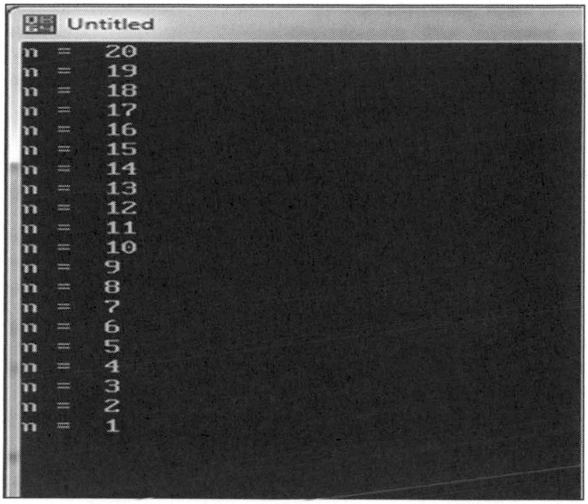

Figure 3.7

Printing numbers in a FOR *loop backwards.*

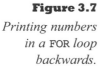

Now for an even bigger example, we'll loop 10 times again, like before, but count the numbers in the loop. This shows that you can *do things* inside the loop other than just printing. Figure 3.8 shows what the program looks like.

```
total = 0
FOR n = 1 to 10
  PRINT "n = "; n
  total = total + n
NEXT
PRINT "Total = "; total
```

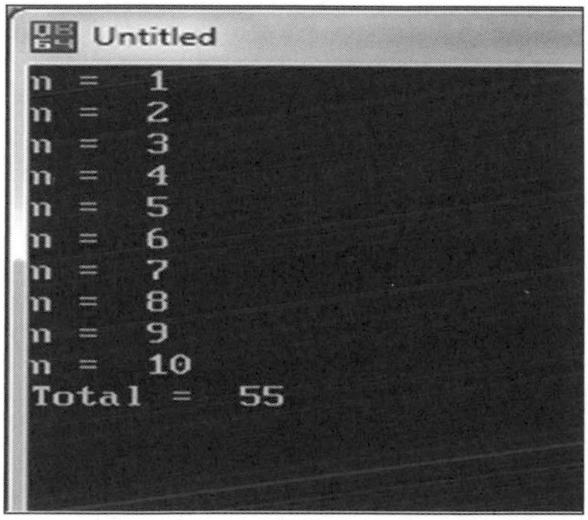

Figure 3.8

Adding up the numbers in the loop.

Let's go back to drawing circles. We can do graphics in a loop too. This program draws 30 circles using a small window in SCREEN mode 13. After the FOR loop, there is no DO loop to keep running and drawing over and over again like we did before when drawing just the one circle. This is a different kind of program that just runs once and then waits to quit. This program does have a loop, but it is not a *real-time loop*. It just runs once and quits.

```
SCREEN 13
FOR n = 1 TO 30
    x = n * 7
    y = n * 3
    r = n * 3
    c = 14
    CIRCLE (x, y), r, c
NEXT
```

The program is shown in Figure 3.9. This program does multiplication for the first time. To multiply numbers together, you use an *asterisk* (*), sometimes called *star*. It is over the 8 key; press Shift+8.

Figure 3.9

Drawing 30 circles using a FOR *loop.*

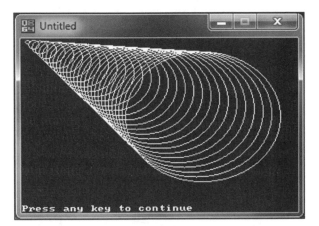

In the line shown below, the looping variable, n, is multiplied by 7.

```
x = n * 7
```

This is really powerful in computer programming.

You can make a loop between any two numbers, forward or backward, and use that number one at a time.

Just like it is being used here:

```
x = n * 7
```

So, when n = 1, then the computer will insert it into the math problem:

```
x = n * 7
x = 1 * 7
x = 7
```

Next, when n = 2, it will go like this:

```
x = n * 7
x = 2 * 7
x = 14
```

And so on, until the end of the loop, where n = 10:

```
x = n * 7
x = 10 * 7
x = 70
```

The x and y variables tell the circle where to draw. The r variable tells the circle how big it should be. The c variable tells the circle what color to use (0 to 255). Here is the program again for reference:

```
FOR n = 1 TO 30
    x = n * 7
    y = n * 3
    r = n * 3
    c = 14
    CIRCLE (x, y), r, c
NEXT
```

We could just put all these values straight into the CIRCLE command. It's just not as easy to understand this way, but the graphics look the same. This new program has only three lines but it does the same thing as the previous program!

```
FOR n = 1 TO 30
    CIRCLE (n*7,n*3), n*3, 14
NEXT
```

There's another type of loop that runs forever! Do you remember which one it is? Right, it's the DO loop! It repeats the code over and over without any limit! You have already used a DO loop a few times before, but here is a new example that prints out numbers in a special way. When you add a semicolon after a PRINT statement, it keeps printing on the same line. This program adds 1 to a variable called i over and over—forever—and prints it out. See the program in Figure 3.10.

```
i = 0
DO
    i = i + 1
    PRINT i;
LOOP
```

Figure 3.10

Printing numbers in an endless loop.

```
Untitled
5284390   5284399   5284400   5284401   5284410   5284411   5284412   5284413
5284414   5284423   5284424   5284425   5284426   5284435   5284436   5284437
5284438   5284439   5284448   5284449   5284450   5284451   5284452   5284451
5284462   5284463   5284464   5284465   5284464   5284475   5284476   5284477
5284478   5284477   5284488   5284489   5284490   5284491   5284490   5284501
5284502   5284503   5284504   5284513   5284514   5284515   5284516   5284525
5284526   5284527   5284528   5284529   5284538   5284539   5284540   5284541
5284542   5284551   5284552   5284553   5284554   5284555   5284564   5284565
5284566   5284567   5284568   5284567   5284578   5284579   5284580   5284581
5284580   5284591   5284592   5284593   5284594   5284595   5284604   5284605
5284606   5284607   5284616   5284617   5284618   5284619   5284620   5284629
5284630   5284631   5284632   5284633   5284642   5284643   5284644   5284645
5284646   5284645   5284656   5284657   5284658   5284659   5284660   5284661
5284660   5284671   5284672   5284673   5284674   5284675   5284676   5284675
5284686   5284687   5284688   5284689   5284690   5284691   5284700   5284701
5284702   5284703   5284704   5284703   5284714   5284715   5284716   5284717
5284718   5284727   5284728   5284729   5284730   5284731   5284740   5284741
5284742   5284743   5284744   5284753   5284754   5284755   5284756   5284757
5284766   5284767   5284768   5284769   5284770   5284779   5284780   5284781
5284782   5284781   5284792   5284793   5284794   5284795   5284804   5284805
5284806   5284807   5284808   5284817   5284818   5284819   5284820   5284821
5284830   5284831   5284832   5284833   5284834   5284843   5284844   5284845
5284846   5284847   5284856   5284857   5284858   5284859   5284860   5284869
5284870   5284871   5284872   5284873
```

How about drawing circles in an infinite loop? For this to look really cool, we need a new math function. Oh, BASIC is full of awesome math functions. We're just getting started. What we need is a way to draw a bunch of circles at different locations. "Different" in math might be called by a special word: random.

SECRET

Randomness means something you can't predict, because it never repeats.

In BASIC, we can get random numbers using the RND statement. Multiply RND by the biggest number you want it to go up to, like RND * 100. You can use RND to draw a bunch of random circles on the screen. Wow, look at them go! See Figure 3.11.

```
SCREEN 13
RANDOMIZE TIMER
DO
    x = RND * 320
    y = RND * 200
    r = RND * 10 + 5
    c = RND * 256
    CIRCLE (x, y), r, c
LOOP
```

Figure 3.11

Drawing circles in an endless (real-time) loop.

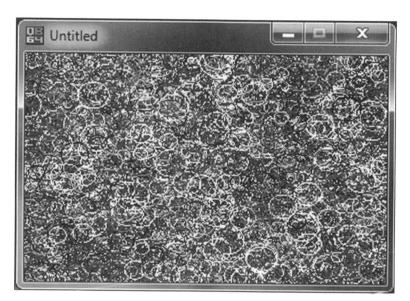

Filling with Colors

Let's look at some new graphics statements. You can fill in a shape on the screen using PAINT. It will fill any shape with a color as long as you know the color of the shape's border.

There are three parameters to the PAINT statement:

```
PAINT (x,y), fillcolor, bordercolor
```

fillcolor is the color you want to fill the shape with.

bordercolor is the color of the boundary around the edges of a shape.

We'll go back to using the larger window. I just wanted you to see how easy it is to do graphics with SCREEN 13. The window is so tiny, though, that it's not very useful for a game. So, this next program will go back to using the 800 × 600 window.

Here is a program that draws a filled circle with the color green (0, 255, 0). It is shown in Figure 3.12.

```
SCREEN _NEWIMAGE(800, 600, 32)
CIRCLE (400, 300), 200, _RGB(255, 255, 255)
PAINT (400, 300), _RGB(0, 255, 0), _RGB(255, 255, 255)
```

Figure 3.12

Drawing a large filled circle with PAINT.

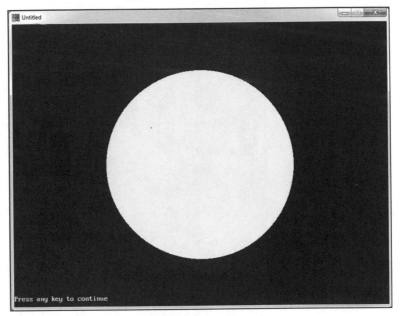

Let's create a more ambitious version of this that draws a bunch of filled circles. But here's the catch—instead of just drawing them all at once, only one circle will draw at a time inside the DO loop. This one is really fun to watch while running! See Figure 3.13.

```
SCREEN _NEWIMAGE(800, 600, 32)
RANDOMIZE TIMER
DO
    x = 50 + RND * 700
    y = 50 + RND * 500
    r = 10 + RND * 40
    red = RND * 256
    grn = RND * 256
    blu = RND * 256
    CIRCLE (x, y), r, _RGB(red, grn, blu)
    PAINT (x, y), _RGB(red, grn, blu), _RGB(red, grn, blu)
    _DISPLAY
LOOP UNTIL INKEY$ = CHR$(27)
SYSTEM
```

Figure 3.13

Drawing filled circles in a real-time loop.

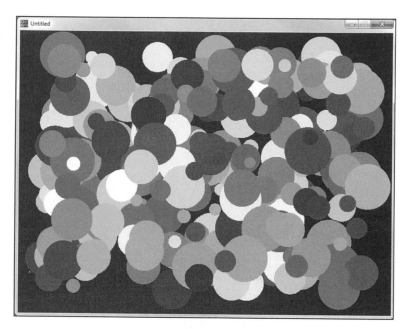

Drawing Lines and Boxes

We can also draw lines and boxes using the LINE statement.

The format of the LINE statement is:

```
LINE (x1,y1)-(x2,y2), color
```

When you draw a line, you have to tell it where the two end points are on the screen. The LINE statement uses a special format for this, with the points in parentheses and a dash between them, followed by a color parameter. It's a little different from CIRCLE. To help show how to use this statement, see Figure 3.14.

Let's write a sample to learn how to draw lines. The program is shown in Figure 3.15.

```
SCREEN _NEWIMAGE(800, 600, 32)
LINE (100, 200)-(600, 500), _RGB(255, 0, 0)
```

Figure 3.14

Diagram of a line showing the two end points.

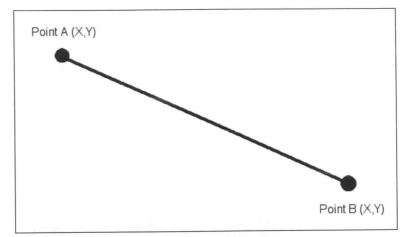

Figure 3.14

Diagram of a line showing the two end points.

Figure 3.15

Drawing a single line with LINE.

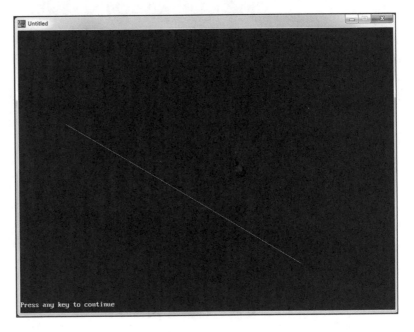

Figure 3.15

Drawing a single line with LINE.

A box is easy to draw using the LINE statement. Just add , B to the end (with the comma). The two points (x1,y1)-(x2,y2) define the upper-left and lower-right corners of the box.

```
LINE (100, 200)-(600, 500), _RGB(255, 0, 0), B
```

This version of LINE draws just the border or edge of a box. To draw a *filled box*, add BF to the end of the statement like this:

```
LINE (100, 200)-(600, 500), _RGB(255, 0, 0), BF
```

This version of LINE draws a filled box, and it's shown in Figure 3.16.

Figure 3.16

Drawing a filled box with the LINE statement.

Drawing Points

We can draw just one little point with the PSET statement. Just specify the position (x,y) and color. Here is a quick example using SCREEN 13. The program is shown in Figure 3.17.

```
SCREEN 13
PSET (150,100), _RGB(200,0,200)
```

It's kind of hard to see just one point, so let's draw a whole bunch of spots. The following program, shown in Figure 3.18, draws random points inside a square on the screen. This looks kind of like an old-fashioned TV channel with no signal.

```
SCREEN 13
DO
    x = 50 + RND * 100
    y = 50 + RND * 100
    c = RND * 256
    PSET (x, y), c
LOOP
```

Figure 3.17

Drawing a single point.

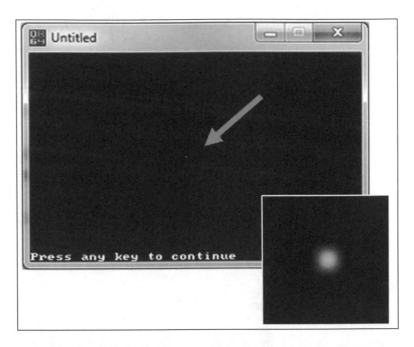

Figure 3.18

Drawing a whole bunch of random points.

Save the Hangman

I'm going to show you a complete game with graphics. This game has some BASIC code that you've never seen before, so it will be a learning experience, but also a bit hard to understand. Use this as an opportunity to learn some new things before you have fully studied them! You can see what the game looks like in Figure 3.19.

Figure 3.19

The "Save the Hangman" game!

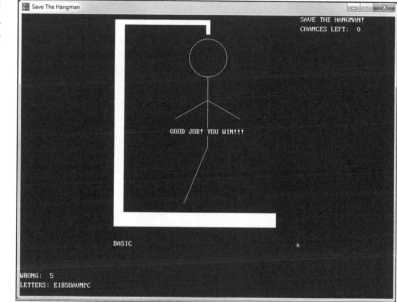

 Go ahead and change the guess word in the Hangman game to any word you want! Just be sure it's just one word—it doesn't like spaces.

This is a pretty big game—the largest program you have seen so far. So, take your time, study the lines, and type them in carefully. Every few minutes you might want to save the program. When you're done, go ahead and change the word$ = "basic" using your own word and then have your friends try to guess it! But, there is one requirement: be sure to only use lowercase letters in word$. Second requirement: don't use any spaces, just use one word. I know it's kind of a shame that we can't make long phrases, but this is how the game works. If you type in any spaces, there will be no way to win because the game doesn't look for the Space key.

```
_TITLE "Save the Hangman"
SCREEN _NEWIMAGE(800, 600, 32)
_SCREENMOVE _MIDDLE
White& = _RGB(255, 255, 255)
Green& = _RGB(0, 255, 0)
letters$ = ""
word$ = "basic" 'use only lowercase
correct$ = STRING$(LEN(word$), "_")
wrong = 0

DO
    CLS

    'draw the platform
    LINE (200, 420)-(550, 450), White&, BF
    LINE (200, 10)-(220, 420), White&, BF
    LINE (200, 10)-(400, 20), White&, BF
    LINE (396, 10)-(404, 40), White&, BF
    'draw the hangman
    IF wrong > 0 THEN CIRCLE (400, 90), 40, Green&
    IF wrong > 1 THEN LINE (400, 130)-(400, 280), Green&
    IF wrong > 2 THEN LINE (400, 180)-(330, 220), Green&
    IF wrong > 3 THEN LINE (400, 180)-(470, 220), Green&
    IF wrong > 4 THEN LINE (400, 280)-(350, 400), Green&
    IF wrong > 5 THEN LINE (400, 280)-(450, 400), Green&

    _PRINTSTRING (600, 0), "SAVE THE HANGMAN!"
    chances = 6 - wrong
    _PRINTSTRING (600, 20), "CHANCES LEFT: " + STR$(chances)

    _PRINTSTRING (200, 480), correct$
    IF UCASE$(word$) = correct$ THEN
        _PRINTSTRING (320, 240), "GOOD JOB! YOU WIN!!!"
    END IF
    IF wrong > 5 THEN
        _PRINTSTRING (300, 240), "OH NO, HANGMAN! YOU LOSE!!"
    END IF
    _PRINTSTRING (0, 550), "WRONG: " + STR$(wrong)
    _PRINTSTRING (0, 570), "LETTERS: " + UCASE$(letters$)

    _DISPLAY
```

```
    k$ = INKEY$
    IF k$ <> "" THEN
        IF k$ >= "a" AND k$ <= "z" THEN
            letters$ = letters$ + k$
            found = 0
            'look for a match
            FOR n = 1 TO LEN(word$)
                c$ = MID$(word$, n, 1)
                IF k$ = c$ THEN
                    MID$(correct$, n, 1) = UCASE$(k$)
                    found = 1
                END IF
            NEXT n
            IF found = 0 THEN wrong = wrong + 1
        END IF
    END IF
LOOP UNTIL k$ = CHR$(27)
SYSTEM
```

Summary

That's the end of your lesson on graphics programming. This is a really fun subject, so we'll definitely do more of it in the next chapter. Speaking of the next chapter, it has something to do with Pirate Treasure!

Quiz

Here is a little quiz to test whether you were paying attention. Try to answer the questions without looking up the answers first. This is not graded; it will just tell you whether you are ready to go to Chapter 4 or not. The answers are found in Appendix A.

1. What command creates a graphics window for a program?

A. SCREEN

B. GRAPHICS

C. WINDOW

D. CLS

2. What command creates a new image of any size you want?

A. GRAPHICS

B. _NEWIMAGE

C. IMAGE

D. NEW_IMAGE

3. What command clears the screen?

A. WIPE

B. CLEAR

C. CLS

D. ERASE

4. What command makes colors?

A. CLR

B. COLOR

C. R_G_B

D. _RGB

5. Which command gets a key press?

A. INKEY$

B. OUTKEY$

C. PINKEY$

D. DINKEY$

Homework

Your homework for this chapter is required to really prove that you understand what you learned! If you have a hard time with this homework, then maybe you went too fast and might need to review the chapter again.

Instructions:

The Hangman game is a pretty big game already, but we can make some improvements to it. Change the game so that the hangman's body (head, torso, arms, legs) is drawn with all different colors instead of just the same color.

Chapter 4

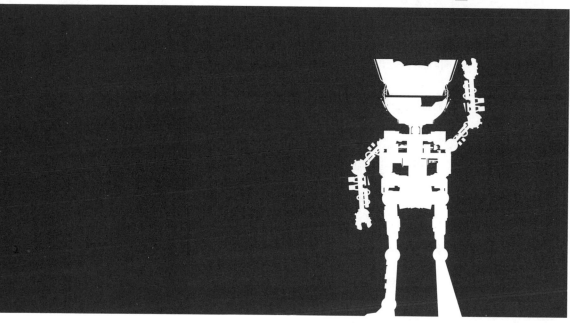

Captain Dread's Secret Pirate Treasure

I'll bet you are starting to feel pretty good about programming in BASIC at this point. It is important to learn the BASIC language so you know what statements you can use in your programs. In this chapter, you will learn more about a real-time loop, and timing, and more graphics. Timing is very important in video games! The game you will be making is called Pirate Treasure. The goal of this game is to pick up all the buried treasure on the island before the time runs out! While making this game, you will learn about sub-procedures.

Using Timers

A timer is like a stopwatch that knows how to keep track of time. When you push the start button on a stopwatch, it starts counting seconds and milliseconds (one-thousandth of a second). When you push the stop button on a stopwatch, then it freezes the timer and shows the current time elapsed. Athletes use stopwatches to time themselves running or swimming laps. Race car drivers use stopwatches to record their lap time around a race track. We use timers for all kinds of things in video game programming. In the Pirate Treasure game, we use a timer that counts down, and you have to get all the treasure before the timer runs out!

A timer keeps track of the seconds going by since it was started. The simplest way to do this is with the TIMER function, which returns the number of seconds since midnight. Here is an example of using TIMER (the hard way). The program looks like Figure 4.1 when you run it.

```
start = TIMER
DO
    IF TIMER - start >= 1 THEN
        PRINT "Timer: "; TIMER
        start = TIMER
    END IF
LOOP UNTIL INKEY$ = CHR$(27)
```

Another way to count seconds is with the TIMER ON statement. When you use this along with a couple of other things, BASIC automatically starts counting. Let's look at the three steps involved.

Figure 4.1

This timer counts one second at a time.

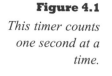

```
Untitled                                              ▢ ▢ ✕
Timer:   57189.07
Timer:   57190.11
Timer:   57191.15
Timer:   57192.2
Timer:   57193.24
Timer:   57194.29
Timer:   57195.33
Timer:   57196.38
Timer:   57197.42
Timer:   57198.46
Timer:   57199.5
Timer:   57200.55
Timer:   57201.59




Press any key to continue
```

SECRET

When finished, this program is called Timer.bas.

First, you have to ask BASIC for a timer using the _FREETIMER statement.

```
t = _FREETIMER
```

Next, you have to use ON TIMER to tell BASIC that you want it to run a sub-procedure when the timer is ready with a new second. This is a little bit complex to set up, so just pay attention to the example and you'll get it.

```
ON TIMER(t, 1) PrintDateTime
```

These two statements tell BASIC that you want it to run a sub-procedure called PrintDateTime when the timer is ready with a new second. Then, the next line turns on the timer.

```
TIMER(t) ON
```

These three lines together create the timer and start it running. This is like clicking the "Start" button on a stopwatch.

Let's finish this program: Type those first three timer lines into a new BASIC program. Then add this:

```
DO
    LOCATE 1, 1
    COLOR 10
    PRINT TIMER
LOOP UNTIL INKEY$ = CHR$(27)
```

Here is the last part of the program, which is a SUB. You use SUB to define a sub-procedure. This is like a mini program that runs all by itself whenever it's called. In this program you're writing right now, the PrintDateTime sub-procedure is called by the timer, so we want it to print out something. How about the date and time?

```
SUB PrintDateTime
LOCATE 3, 1
COLOR 11
PRINT "Date: "; DATE$
PRINT "Time: "; TIME$
END SUB
```

 SECRET When finished, this program is called OnTimer.bas. You can find this program in the files that go with the book (www.courseptr.com/downloads).

When you run the program, it looks like this (see Figure 4.2).

There were some new statements in this program you haven't seen before. The LOCATE statement causes the cursor to move to a specific place on the screen. The COLOR statement changes the text color to one of the 16 standard colors, which are:

0 - Black	8 - Gray
1 - Blue	9 - Bright Blue
2 - Green	10 - Bright Green
3 - Cyan	11 - Bright Cyan
4 - Red	12 - Bright Red
5 - Purple	13 - Bright Purple
6 - Brown	14 - Yellow
7 - White	15 - Bright White

Figure 4.2

Using ON TIMER *to create an automatic stopwatch.*

Using Sub-Procedures

As you just learned, a SUB statement defines a sub-procedure. This is like a mini program *within* your program. It can have its own variables and do anything that a regular program does. But, usually you don't want to create a window and run a game inside a SUB, because the regular program is also still running.

Think of a SUB as a pit stop for a race car that needs gas: the driver goes into the pit stop, and the pit crew changes the tires and fills up the gas tank, then the driver takes off again around the race track. That's like a SUB. The driver isn't doing anything while the pit crew is working on the car; he or she just sits there and waits for a minute. The driver is like the main program, waiting for the SUB to finish, which means the SUB is like a pit crew: it has a job to do, and when it's done, the main program (the driver) takes over again.

Below is a program that uses a sub-procedure called PrintAt. This SUB makes it easier to print words anywhere on the screen in any color you want by just calling it with parameters. For example, if you want to print "Hello" at the upper-left corner of the screen, you do it like this:

```
PrintAt 1, 1, 10, "Hello"
```

Here is the code for a bigger example. This program is called ILoveBasic.bas.

```
FOR n = 1 TO 100
    x = RND * 70 + 1
    y = RND * 45 + 1
    c = RND * 16
    PrintAt x, y, c, "I love BASIC!"
NEXT n

SUB PrintAt (X, Y, C, text$)
LOCATE Y, X
COLOR C
PRINT text$
END SUB
```

Here is what the program looks like when you run it (see Figure 4.3).

Figure 4.3

Printing words all over the screen using a SUB.

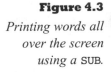

Let's try another example. The next program draws a rotating circle using trigonometry (advanced math).

```
_TITLE "Rotating Circle"
SCREEN _NEWIMAGE(800, 600, 32)
blue& = _RGB(0, 0, 255)
angle = 0
DO
    CLS
    angle = angle + 0.5
    x = 400 + COS(angle * 3.14 / 180) * 200
    y = 300 + SIN(angle * 3.14 / 180) * 200

    FillCircle x, y, 100, blue&
```

```
       _DISPLAY
LOOP UNTIL INKEY$ = CHR$(27)
SYSTEM


SUB FillCircle (X, Y, Rad, Col)
CIRCLE (X, Y), Rad, Col
PAINT (X, Y), Col
END SUB
```

This is a pretty neat program. Go ahead and run it after you type it in. This program is called RotatingCircle.bas. When you run it, it will look like Figure 4.4.

Figure 4.4

Drawing a circle rotating around the center of the window.

There's a lot of code in the Rotating Circle program that hasn't been explained. It's a bit much to learn all at once, since this chapter already covers a lot. So, how about a quick summary? The two lines that set the x and y variables use trigonometry functions to calculate the position of the circle around the center of the screen. The functions Sine (SIN) and Cosine (COS) help to do this calculation. The 3.14 / 180 part converts degrees to radians (since all trigonometry uses radians). This kind of code is very common in video games.

You can do anything you want in a SUB, not just printing. But, if you want to compute something and get an answer, then that calls for a bird of a different feature—a *function*.

Using Functions

A function is a SUB that sends an answer back to you. Programmers call the answer a *return value*. Functions are really helpful! A function returns one value, and only one. Let's write a short program to show how to use a function. This program, which is called AddFunction.bas, has you enter two numbers. Then a function called Add( ) adds the numbers together and returns the answer.

 A FUNCTION sends an answer back (a return value), but a SUB does not.

```
INPUT "Enter number 1: "; number1
INPUT "Enter number 2: "; number2
answer = Add(number1, number2)
PRINT number1; "+"; number2; "="; answer

FUNCTION Add (A, B)
sum = A + B
Add = sum
END FUNCTION
```

Here is the output when you run the program. I entered 12 and 16 as the numbers, and it computed the answer as 28.

```
Enter number 1: ? 12
Enter number 2: ? 16
 12 + 16 = 28
```

You don't have to just do math in a function; you can also do words (strings). Here is another example that has you enter your first and last name, and then a function called Combine$( ) returns the names with a space between them. One thing you'll notice is the Combine$( ) function has a dollar sign at the end. This tells BASIC to send back a text string, not a number. Functions send back numbers by default.

```
INPUT "What is your first name"; first$
INPUT "What is your last name"; last$
fullname$ = Combine(first$, last$)
PRINT "Hello, "; fullname$; "."

FUNCTION Combine$ (A$, B$)
both$ = A$ + " " + B$
Combine$ = both$
END FUNCTION
```

Here is the output when you run the program. Try it yourself! This program is called CombineFunction.bas.

```
What is your first name? Tony
What is your last name? Stark
Hello, Tony Stark.
```

There's no rule that you have to use the same type of variable in the parameters and return value. They can be different.

The Pirate Treasure Game

Now you will learn how to make the biggest example game yet! This game is called Pirate Treasure! The character on the screen is a pirate that *you* get to control with the arrow keys (Up, Down, Left, and Right). You have to move the pirate to the treasure chest before the timer runs out. You have 30 seconds! Every time you run the game, the pirate and treasure start off in a different place on the desert island.

This is the *biggest* game you have programmed in BASIC so far; it's huge! Are you ready to start typing it in? If not, you can load the game file; it's called PirateTreasure.bas. Let me explain the game to you. When you run the game, it comes up like the screen shown in Figure 4.5.

Using the arrow keys, move the pirate on the island, but *stay away from the ocean!* If you touch the ocean, the pirate will drown and you will lose (Figure 4.6).

Figure 4.5

The Pirate Treasure game.

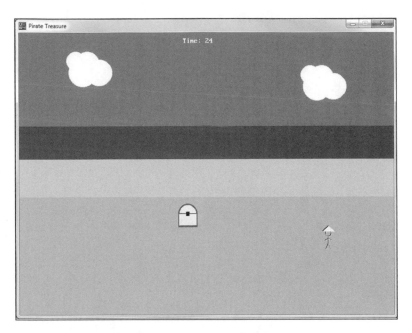

Figure 4.6

Don't go too far away from the shore or you will drown!

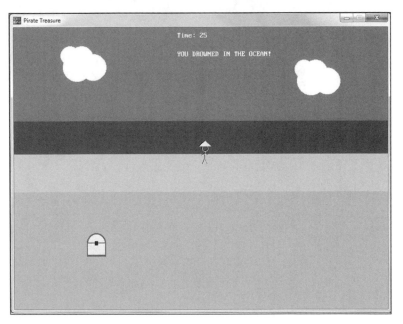

But, if you're careful to avoid the ocean currents, and move fast enough, you just might make it to the pirate treasure, and then you win! If this happens, the game will open the treasure chest and tell you how much gold you found! This is based on how long it takes you to get the treasure chest—if you get to it faster, you get more gold! The win screen is shown in Figure 4.7. Have fun typing in the game code and be sure to save it.

Figure 4.7

You got the treasure!

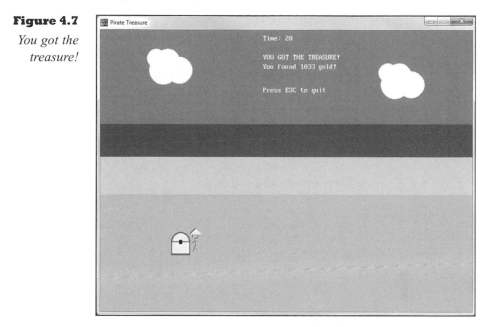

```
_TITLE "Pirate Treasure"

DIM SHARED scrn&, island&, cloud&, pirate&, treasure&
DIM SHARED white&, black&, green&, gold&, brown&, sky&,
darksand&, sand&
DIM SHARED ocean&, counter

RANDOMIZE TIMER

scrn& = _NEWIMAGE(800, 600, 32)
SCREEN scrn&
CALL MakeColors
CALL MakeIsland

CALL MakeCloud
```

```
CALL MakePirate
pirate_x = 10 + RND * 700
pirate_y = 280 + RND * 220

CALL MakeTreasure
treasure_x = 10 + RND * 700
treasure_y = 280 + RND * 220

'start a stopwatch timer
t = _FREETIMER
ON TIMER(t, 1) CountDown
TIMER(t) ON
counter = 31

_DEST display&
gameover$ = "false"

DO
    CLS
    _PUTIMAGE (0, 0), island&, scrn&
    _PUTIMAGE (100, 40), cloud&, scrn&
    _PUTIMAGE (600, 70), cloud&, scrn&
    _PUTIMAGE (treasure_x, treasure_y), treasure&, scrn&
    _PUTIMAGE (pirate_x, pirate_y), pirate&, scrn&
    _PRINTMODE _KEEPBACKGROUND
    _PRINTSTRING (350, 10), "Time:" + STR$(counter)
    k$ = INKEY$
    IF k$ <> "" THEN
        code = ASC(k$)
        IF code = 0 THEN
            code = ASC(k$, 2)
            IF code = 72 THEN 'move up
                pirate_y = pirate_y - 5
            ELSEIF code = 80 THEN 'move down
                pirate_y = pirate_y + 5
            ELSEIF code = 75 THEN 'move left
                pirate_x = pirate_x - 5
            ELSEIF code = 77 THEN 'move right
                pirate_x = pirate_x + 5
            END IF
        ELSE
            IF k$ = CHR$(27) THEN gameover$ = "true"
        END IF
    END IF

    'see if you got the treasure
    px = pirate_x + 30
    py = pirate_y + 30
    IF px > treasure_x AND py > treasure_y THEN
```

```
            IF px < treasure_x + 60 AND py < treasure_y + 60 THEN
                _PRINTSTRING (350, 50), "YOU GOT THE TREASURE!"
                gold = INT((30 - counter) * 100 + RND * 100)
                _PRINTSTRING (350, 70), "You found" + STR$(gold) ↵
+ " gold!"
                _PRINTSTRING (350, 120), "Press ESC to quit"
                gameover$ = "true"
            END IF
        END IF
        IF py < 270 THEN
            _PRINTSTRING (350, 50), "YOU DROWNED IN THE OCEAN!"
            gameover$ = "true"
        END IF

    _DISPLAY

LOOP UNTIL gameover$ = "true"
DO
    _DISPLAY
LOOP UNTIL INKEY$ = CHR$(27)
SYSTEM

SUB CountDown ()
counter = counter - 1
END SUB

SUB MakeColors ()
white& = _RGB(255, 255, 255)
black& = _RGB(0, 0, 0)
green& = _RGB(0, 255, 0)
gold& = _RGB(255, 215, 0)
brown& = _RGB(100, 100, 40)
sky& = _RGB(110, 110, 240)
darksand& = _RGB(214, 165, 116)
sand& = _RGB(234, 185, 136)
ocean& = _RGB(60, 60, 240)
END SUB

SUB MakePirate ()
pirate& = _NEWIMAGE(60, 60)
_DEST pirate&
'make the pirate's shadow
LINE (7, 11)-(19, 0), black&
LINE (19, 1)-(31, 11), black&
LINE (7, 11)-(31, 11), black&
PAINT (19, 9), black&
CIRCLE (19, 16), 6, black&
```

```
LINE (19, 23)-(19, 37), black&
LINE (19, 27)-(12, 31), black&
LINE (19, 27)-(26, 31), black&
LINE (19, 37)-(14, 49), black&
LINE (19, 37)-(24, 49), black&
'draw the pirate
LINE (8, 12)-(20, 1), green&
LINE (20, 1)-(32, 12), green&
LINE (8, 12)-(32, 12), green&
PAINT (20, 10), green&
CIRCLE (20, 17), 6, green&
LINE (20, 24)-(20, 38), green&
LINE (20, 28)-(13, 32), green&
LINE (20, 28)-(27, 32), green&
LINE (20, 38)-(15, 50), green&
LINE (20, 38)-(25, 50), green&
END SUB

SUB MakeTreasure ()
treasure& = _NEWIMAGE(60, 60)
_DEST treasure&
CIRCLE (20, 20), 20, brown&
PAINT (20, 10), brown&
CIRCLE (20, 20), 17, gold&
PAINT (20, 20), gold&
LINE (0, 20)-(40, 49), brown&, BF
LINE (2, 22)-(38, 45), gold&, BF
LINE (17, 17)-(23, 25), black&, BF
END SUB

SUB MakeIsland ()
island& = _NEWIMAGE(800, 600)
_DEST island&
LINE (0, 0)-(799, 200), sky&, BF
LINE (0, 200)-(799, 270), ocean&, BF
LINE (0, 270)-(799, 350), sand&, BF
LINE (0, 350)-(799, 599), darksand&, BF
END SUB

SUB MakeCloud ()
cloud& = _NEWIMAGE(100, 100)
_DEST cloud&
CIRCLE (20, 20), 20, white&
PAINT (20, 20), white&
CIRCLE (45, 25), 25, white&
PAINT (45, 30), white&
CIRCLE (70, 45), 28, white&
PAINT (70, 45), white&
```

```
CIRCLE (35, 45), 30, white&
PAINT (35, 60), white&
END SUB
```

Summary

You learned some very important things about BASIC programming in this chapter! You learned about timers, sub-procedures, functions, and even more graphics. You might not have even realized it, but in the Pirate Treasure game, you were using bitmaps to draw the shapes in the game.

Quiz

Here is a little quiz to test whether you were paying attention. Try to answer the questions without looking up the answers first. This is not graded; it will just tell you whether you are ready to go to the next chapter. The answers are found in Appendix A.

1. Which command gets the time in seconds since midnight?

A. SECONDS

B. TIMER

C. GET_TIME

D. TIME_SECONDS

2. Which command gets the current date as a string?

A. CURRENT_DATE

B. DATE

C. DATE$

D. GET_DATE$

3. Which command gets the current time as a string?

A. TIME$

B. TIME

C. GET_TIME$

D. CURRENT_TIME

4. What statement starts a sub-procedure?

A. SHIP

B. AIRPLANE

C. TORPEDO

D. SUB

5. What statement starts a function?

A. FUNCTION

B. FUNC

C. FN

D. STATEMENT

Homework

Your homework for this chapter is required in order to really prove that you understand what you learned! If you have a hard time with this homework, then maybe you went too fast and might need to review the chapter again.

Instructions:

Using the custom Add() function demonstrated in this chapter as an example, write your own function called Multiply() that will return two numbers multiplied by each other. The math operator for doing multiplication is * (asterisk).

Chapter 5

Cannonball Carl and the Castle Crashers

This chapter is all about using the mouse for player input in a game. You will learn how to get the mouse coordinates and draw a shape on the screen that moves with the mouse. You will use this idea to make a game where you get to shoot your cannon at bad guys hiding in their castle. To make a realistic castle, you will learn about arrays and data. You will use DATA statements that tell the game how the castle should look, and then draw the castle accordingly. This is a very early form of level design. Level design is all about designing levels for video games. Some people are really good at it and design game levels every day. Wouldn't it be great to get paid to work on video games?

Tracking the Mouse

To get the status of the mouse, all you have to do is use a statement called _MOUSEINPUT, which returns 0 if there's an error reading the mouse (which shouldn't happen unless you unplug your mouse).

```
mouse = _MOUSEINPUT
```

You won't need to use the mouse variable after this line, but _MOUSEINPUT does need to send an answer so it's required.

Once you have read the mouse, then you can get the mouse position and button inputs.

The _MOUSEX function indicates the horizontal (X) position, while _MOUSEY indicates the current vertical (Y) position.

The _MOUSEWHEEL function tells whether the mouse wheel is being moved, either up or down.

The _MOUSEBUTTON function tells you which mouse button is being pressed.

Here is a short example to show you how to get mouse input. Since this program runs in text mode, the mouse coordinates are in text positions—which is pretty cool!

```
_TITLE "Mouse Demo"
DO
    mouse = _MOUSEINPUT
    mouse_x = _MOUSEX
    mouse_y = _MOUSEY
    LOCATE 5, 32
```

```
        COLOR 11
        PRINT "MOUSE XY ="; mouse_x; mouse_y
LOOP UNTIL INKEY$ = CHR$(27)
```

Make sure to use _MOUSEINPUT *every time* you need to read from the mouse. That means, above any code that uses the mouse, like _MOUSEX and _MOUSEY. If you don't call _MOUSEINPUT first, then the mouse won't update correctly.

When you run this little program, the output (shown in Figure 5.1) shows the mouse cursor position with decimal values, but you only really need to pay attention to the whole number on the left of the decimal.

Figure 5.1

Reporting the mouse position in text mode.

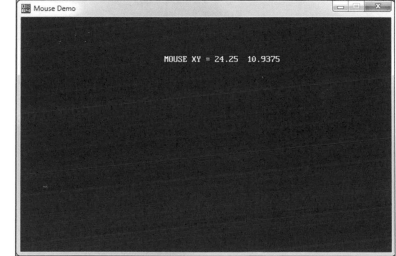

Mouse input in graphics mode is much more interesting because the actual mouse cursor position is returned as a precise pixel location. Here is a version of the above program that runs in graphics mode. When you run the program, it looks like Figure 5.2.

```
_TITLE "Mouse Demo"
SCREEN _NEWIMAGE(800, 600, 32)
DO
    mouse = _MOUSEINPUT
    mouse_x = _MOUSEX
    mouse_y = _MOUSEY
    _PRINTSTRING (300, 200), "MOUSE XY = " +
STR$(mouse_x) + "," + STR$(mouse_y)
LOOP UNTIL INKEY$ = CHR$(27)
```

Figure 5.2

Getting the mouse position in graphics mode.

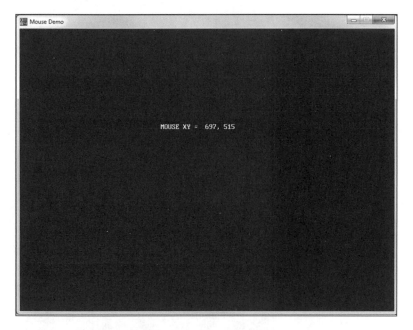

Remember, *every example* in this book uses the Escape key to exit! That's what chr$(27) means: Escape key.

Using Arrays

An array is a container with many slots in it for storing a bunch of things. Each item in the array must be the same as all the other items (that is, the type of item). You can store a bunch of numbers, a bunch of letters, or a bunch of words—but you can't mix them up in the same array.

To create an array, you use the DIM statement. After DIM, enter the name of the array. After the name, then tell BASIC how many slots you need in the array. Like this:

```
DIM names$(10)
```

That one is really neat. It can handle 10 names. Here is how you can put names in the slots:

```
names$(1) = "John"
names$(2) = "Debra"
names$(3) = "Kip"
names$(4) = "Napoleon"
names$(5) = "Grandma"
names$(6) = "Pedro"
names$(7) = "Summer"
names$(8) = "Steve"
names$(9) = "Mr. Tennyson"
names$(10) = "Uncle Rico"
```

Now, when you want to use the names, like to print them out, there's a hard way and an easy way. Let's do it the hard way first. Here is how you print the names the hard way:

```
PRINT names$(1)
PRINT names$(2)
PRINT names$(3)
PRINT names$(4)
PRINT names$(5)
PRINT names$(6)
PRINT names$(7)
PRINT names$(8)
PRINT names$(9)
PRINT names$(10)
```

If you run the program at this point, it will look like this:

```
John
Debra
Kip
Napoleon
Grandma
Pedro
Summer
Steve
Mr. Tennyson
Uncle Rico
```

That's good. But do you really want to have to type PRINT for every single name like that? Forget about it! If you have to type that much all day long, that kills your fingers! That's the hard way to print an array. Let's do it the smart way.

```
FOR n = 1 TO 10
    PRINT names$(n)
NEXT n
```

You can use numbers in an array too. Here's an example that fills a huge array with random numbers and then prints them all out. Just to help make sure you don't get confused about the two loops, the first one uses N, and the second one uses A for the index variable. When you run this program, it will print out 100 random numbers like you can see in Figure 5.3.

```
DIM numbers(101)
FOR N = 1 TO 100
    numbers(N) = RND * 100
NEXT N
FOR A = 1 TO 100
    PRINT numbers(A);
NEXT A
```

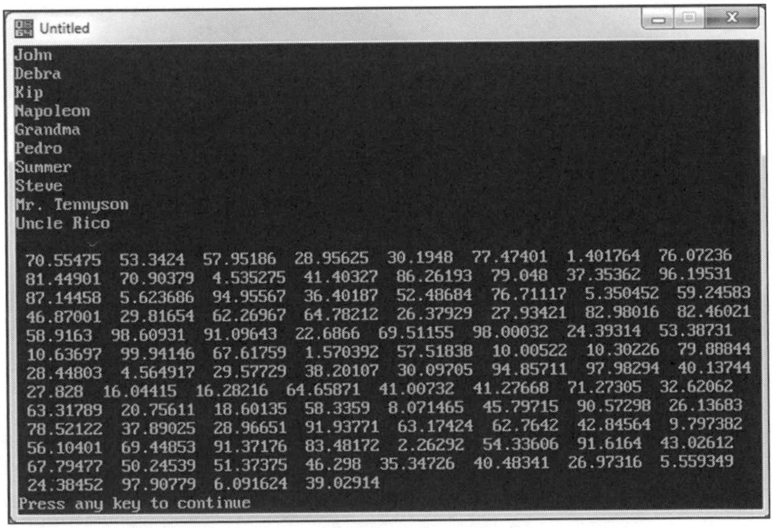

Figure 5.3

Using arrays to store lots of data.

In our game, Cannonball Carl, there is a more complex array with two layers! See if you can understand how it works by examining the code for the game. I'll give you a hint: One layer is for the blocks across (13), and one layer is for the blocks down (5).

Cannonball Carl

Now you are ready to make the game. This is a really exciting game! It's the *biggest* game you have ever made in your entire life! Well, okay, maybe just from this book. But it's huge! There's a lot of code here, and it's all really good code, so go ahead and type it into BASIC, then save it. The file is called CannonballCarl.bas if you wimp out and want to just load it instead. No one will call you a wimp if you wimp out and don't type it in. There's no hand holding here! This is just one big long code listing for an awesome game. Just type it in already!

```
_TITLE "Cannonball Carl"
DATA 1,0,1,0,1,0,1,0,1,0,1,0,1
DATA 1,1,1,1,1,1,1,1,1,1,1,1,1
DATA 1,1,1,1,1,1,1,1,1,1,1,1,1
DATA 1,1,1,1,1,1,1,1,1,1,1,1,1
DATA 1,1,1,1,1,1,1,1,1,1,1,1,1

'read castle data
DIM level(13, 5)
FOR a = 0 TO 4
    FOR b = 0 TO 12
        READ level(b, a)
        PRINT level(b, a);
    NEXT b
NEXT a

scrn& = _NEWIMAGE(800, 600, 32)
SCREEN scrn&

blue& = _RGB(30, 30, 200)
ltblue& = _RGB(30, 30, 250)
steel& = _RGB(159, 182, 205)
wood& = _RGB(133, 94, 66)
red& = _RGB(220, 0, 0)

'create castle bricks
brick& = _NEWIMAGE(60, 60, 32)
```

```
_DEST brick&
LINE (0, 0)-(59, 59), blue&, BF
LINE (0, 0)-(59, 59), ltblue&, B

'create the cannon
cannon& = _NEWIMAGE(60, 60, 32)
_DEST cannon&
LINE (15, 30)-(45, 55), wood&, BF
LINE (0, 40)-(59, 44), wood&, BF
LINE (0, 30)-(6, 55), steel&, BF
LINE (53, 30)-(59, 55), steel&, BF
LINE (24, 0)-(36, 59), steel&, BF
LINE (22, 35)-(38, 59), steel&, BF
cannon_x = 350
cannon_y = 520

'create the cannonball
cannonball& = _NEWIMAGE(24, 24, 32)
_DEST cannonball&
CIRCLE (10, 10), 10, red&
PAINT (10, 10), red&
cannonball_x = 0
cannonball_y = 0
shooting = 0

_DEST scrn&
DO
    CLS

    'draw the castle
    FOR a = 0 TO 4
        FOR b = 0 TO 12
            IF level(b, a) = 1 THEN
                x = 10 + b * 60
                y = 10 + a * 60
                _PUTIMAGE (x, y), brick&, scrn& 'draw
                    one brick

                'see if cannonball hit a block
                IF shooting = 1 THEN
                    cx = cannonball_x + 10
                    cy = cannonball_y + 10
                    IF cx > x AND cx < x + 60 AND cy > ↵
y AND cy < y + 60 THEN
                        shooting = 0
                        level(b, a) = 0 'block hit
                    END IF
                END IF
```

```
                    END IF
                NEXT b
        NEXT a

        'get mouse position
        mouse = _MOUSEINPUT
        cannon_x = _MOUSEX
        IF cannon_x > 740 THEN cannon_x = 740

        'draw the cannon
        _PUTIMAGE (cannon_x, cannon_y), cannon&, scrn&

        'fire cannon!
        IF _MOUSEBUTTON(1) AND shooting = 0 THEN
            shooting = 1
            cannonball_x = cannon_x + 20
            cannonball_y = cannon_y - 20
        END IF

        'draw cannonball
        IF shooting = 1 THEN
            _PUTIMAGE (cannonball_x, cannonball_y), ↵
cannonball&, scrn&
        END IF

        'move cannonball
        cannonball_y = cannonball_y - 2
        IF cannonball_y < 0 THEN
            shooting = 0
        END IF

        'see if the castle is destroyed
        count = 0
        FOR a = 0 TO 4
            FOR b = 0 TO 12
                IF level(b, a) = 1 THEN
                    count = count + 1
                END IF
            NEXT b
        NEXT a
        IF count = 0 THEN
            _PRINTSTRING (300, 300), "YOU TOTALLY HOSED ↵
THE CASTLE!"
            _PRINTSTRING (350, 350), "Y O U    R U L E ! !"
        END IF

        _DISPLAY
LOOP UNTIL INKEY$ = CHR$(27)
```

END

Alrighty then! Are you ready to run the game? Since BASIC is really helpful, you can't really make too many mistakes without it complaining. Have you seen how much BASIC complains if you type in something wrong? It puts up a big bright red bar on the code and it refuses to run until you fix it! Talk about cranky.

Figure 5.4

Shoot cannonballs to destroy the castle!

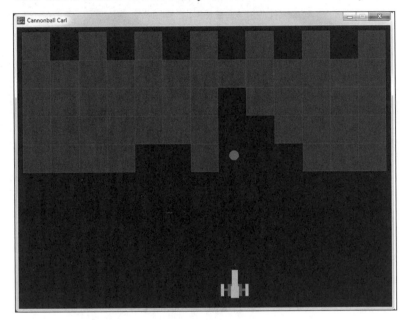

When you run the game, it will look something like Figure 5.4.

If you can blow up the entire castle with your cannon, then you are rewarded with some really great special effects using shaders and 3D rendered fireworks that spell out the words shown in Figure 5.5. Isn't it awesome! You rule!

Oh, what's wrong, you don't see the special effects? Just run the game and you'll see; it prints out something when you win!

Alright, now that we're past all that technical mumbo-jumbo (you know, writing code), it's time to become a *level designer*!

Go back to the top of the program. Look for the lines that begin with the word DATA. There are five lines. If you look carefully, you can tell that they're in the shape of the castle. Every time you see a "1", that's a solid block. Wherever you see a "0", that's an empty space.

Figure 5.5

You destroyed the whole castle. You rule!

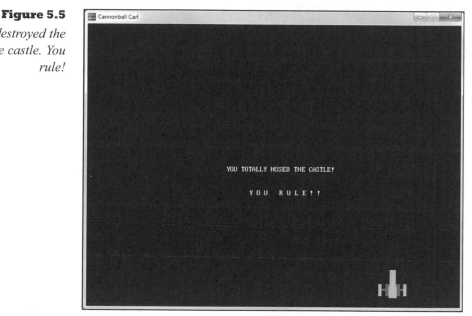

You can design any building or shape you want by changing these numbers. Just make sure to use *overwrite* mode on your keyboard (Insert key), and only change the numbers that are showing. Don't add any more lines or anything, or the game probably will not work right. There are 13 blocks across, and 5 down. That's your level! Go ahead and change it! You're now a level designer!

Summary

This chapter helped you to learn about arrays, mouse input, and even more graphics programming! You are making some pretty serious games already, and we're just finishing up Chapter 5. Forsooth! I'm worried that you might become too awesome and stop reading the rest of the book. So, maybe in the next chapter we'll learn about how libraries work: you know, the card index, the Dewey decimal system, and just for fun, you'll learn about the geography of the country formerly known as Yugoslavia. You love geography, right?

Quiz

Here is a little quiz to test whether you were paying attention. Try to answer the questions without looking up the answers first. This is not graded; it will just tell you whether you are ready to go to the next chapter or not. The answers are found in Appendix A. If you stink at this quiz, then go back and read the chapter again!

1. Which command gets the state of the mouse?

A. _MOUSEINPUT

B. STATE

C. MOUSE

D. EEK

2. What command gets the mouse's X position?

A. MOUSE

B. _MOUSEX

C. MOUSE_X

D. MX

3. What command gets the mouse's Y position?

A. MOUSE_Y

B. MOUSE

C. _MOUSEY

D. MY

4. What command gets the mouse button state?

A. BUTTON

B. MOUSE_B

C. MOUSE_BUTTON

D. _MOUSEBUTTON

5. What statement defines an array variable?

A. DIM

B. ARRAY

C. DEF

D. INT

Homework

Your homework for this chapter is required to really prove that you understand what you learned! If you have a hard time with this homework, then maybe you went too fast and might need to review the chapter again.

Instructions:

The Cannonball Carl game features a level that is defined with DATA statements. Modify the data, designing your own level that looks different from the castle.

Chapter 6

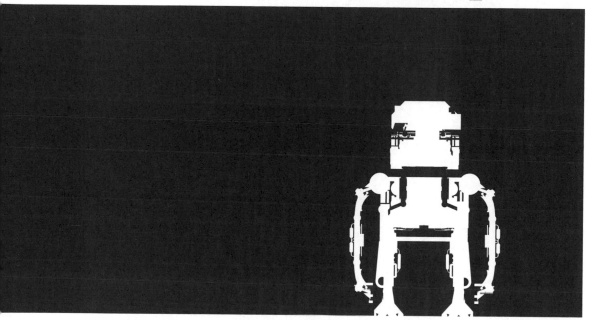

Muscle Man
Backpack Attack

Welcome to the backpack chapter. What does that mean, you wonder? It means you're going to learn about storing things in a BASIC program. This goes along with the previous chapter. Remember Cannonball Carl? That game used an array to keep track of the castle blocks which we described in a level using DATA statements. The castle was built with blocks sort of like LEGOs. That's a very important thing to learn about video games, because almost all of them work this way. There are some things in the Cannonball Carl game that will be explained a little better in this chapter as you make a game called Muscle Man Backpack Attack!

Backpack Attack

This game could be called Backpack Dodgeball, but I like Attack better. In this game, a Muscle Man has invaded your school, and you have to stop him from stealing all the kids' backpacks! So you have to run around and get the backpacks before Muscle Man gets them, and throw apples at him to stun him. Let's face it, as a kid, you don't stand a chance against Muscle Man, so you have to use a projectile. Just pretend the apples are flaming fireballs of molten lead... or something. Actually, that would be really cool!

Alas, we haven't learned to do animation yet, and a fireball that just sits there without, you know, *flaming*, looks really lame—almost worse than an apple. Actually, it's not an apple; all we can muster is a filled-in orange circle. So, pretend the orange circle is an apple, and then pretend the apple is a flaming fireball of molten lead, and throw them at Muscle Man. Come to think of it, an orange circle is more like an *orange* than an apple. So, okay, just pretend the apple is an orange.

Oh, brother! We need some 3D models. If you have 3ds max, can you just make a model of an orange or an apple, then write some BASIC code to load the model and draw it instead of the circle?

No? Okay, never mind, just use the orange circle.

By the way, the backpacks are brown squares. Just saying.

So, let's get started making this sweet game. First of all, let's go over the rules. You are the kid. You move the kid left and right with the Left and Right arrow keys.

As the kid, you are allowed to throw orange apples to stun the Muscle Man. Press Z to throw left, or X to throw right. I recommend using your left hand to throw orange apples, and your right hand to move the kid back and forth. If you try to do the moving with your left hand, and the throwing with your right, your hands will be all tangled up. It's like this for a reason. Wait, let's just show all the controls here in Table 6.1.

Table 6.1	Backpack Attack Controls
Key	**Action**
Left	Move kid left
Right	Move kid right
Z	Shoot left
X	Shoot right

Let's see what the game looks like (see Figure 6.1).

Figure 6.1

The Backpack Attack game has some sweet graphics. You control the blue stick figure on the left.

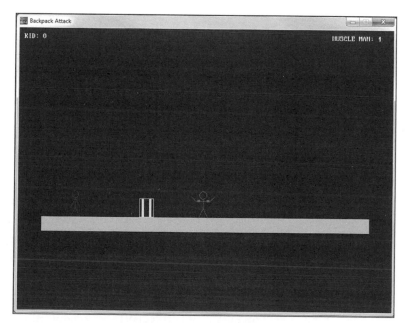

Making the Graphics

This is going to be a sweet game, but it's kind of big, so let's go over it in stages so you can rest your brain every few minutes. The first step of the game is to initialize everything. That means, create all the graphics used in the game. It's called programmer art when you let a programmer do the artwork for a game. If we had an artist from *Plants vs. Zombies*, then the game would have better artwork. We could make Muscle Man into the football zombie, and the kid into, like, a sunflower.

First, let's do the screen and colors.

```
_TITLE "Backpack Attack"

scrn& = _NEWIMAGE(800, 600, 32)
SCREEN scrn&
green& = _RGB(20, 220, 20)
blue& = _RGB(20, 20, 230)
ltblue& = _RGB(30, 30, 250)
red& = _RGB(220, 20, 20)
yellow& = _RGB(220, 220, 20)
wood& = _RGB(133, 94, 66)
orange& = _RGB(255, 127, 0)
white& = _RGB(255, 255, 255)
```

Next up is the code to make the kid. Don't laugh, he's already going to have a hard time against Muscle Man. Believe in him!

```
'make the kid
kid& = _NEWIMAGE(40, 60, 32)
_DEST kid&
CIRCLE (20, 12), 7, blue&
LINE (20, 20)-(20, 40), blue&
LINE (20, 20)-(10, 40), blue&
LINE (20, 20)-(30, 40), blue&
LINE (20, 40)-(10, 60), blue&
LINE (20, 40)-(30, 60), blue&
kid_x = 100
kid_y = 340
die$ = "false"
gameover$ = "false"
kid_score = 0
```

Next, we will make the Muscle Man. He's a pretty good bad guy. The only problem is, it's easy to stun him with just an apple. So, he needs to learn some moves.

```
'make the muscle man
muscle& = _NEWIMAGE(80, 80, 32)
_DEST muscle&
CIRCLE (40, 12), 8, red&
LINE (40, 20)-(40, 40), red&
LINE (40, 25)-(25, 25), red&
LINE (28, 22)-(33, 26), red&, BF
LINE (25, 25)-(15, 15), red&
LINE (40, 25)-(55, 25), red&
LINE (48, 22)-(53, 26), red&, BF
LINE (55, 25)-(65, 15), red&
LINE (40, 40)-(30, 60), red&
LINE (40, 40)-(50, 60), red&
muscle_x = 600
muscle_y = 340
stunned = 0
muscle_score = 0
```

Next, we will make the backpack. This looks like a real backpack too! Are you typing this code into BASIC (i.e., QB64)? Just type it in exactly how it appears in order here. I'm just pausing to let your brain rest every few minutes, remember? If you want to just hurry up and type it all in, go ahead.

```
'make the backpack
backpack& = _NEWIMAGE(40, 40, 32)
_DEST backpack&
LINE (5, 0)-(35, 39), yellow&, B
LINE (10, 0)-(14, 39), yellow&, BF
LINE (30, 0)-(26, 39), yellow&, BF
bp_x = 300
bp_y = 10
```

Now for the apple. It's an orange apple, so obviously it's got an identity crisis.

```
'make the "apple"
apple& = _NEWIMAGE(10, 10, 32)
_DEST apple&
CIRCLE (5, 5), 4, orange&
PAINT (5, 5), orange&
apple_x = 0
apple_y = 0
throwing$ = "false"
apple_dir = 0
```

Making the Game Loop

There, all the graphics are done! Now, it's time for the nitty gritty, the meat and potatoes; what I'm referring to, of course, is the game loop! Now, here's the deal with the game loop: It's made out of a DO loop. So, while you're typing in this code, it's helpful to add the LOOP part after the DO part, so BASIC doesn't freak out. It doesn't like code that's broken, even if you're still typing it in. Kind of impatient. But, anyway, here's all the code for the game loop, which is what makes the game actually work.

First of all, let's go over the code to draw a few things: the level and the kid.

```
_DEST scrn&
DO
    CLS

    'draw the level
    LINE (50, 400)-(750, 430), green&, BF

    'draw the kid
    IF kid_x < 50 OR kid_x > 750 THEN die$ = "true"
    IF die$ = "true" THEN
        _PRINTSTRING (kid_x, 350), "AHHH!!!"
        kid_y = kid_y + 0.5
        IF kid_y > 600 THEN gameover$ = "true"
    END IF
    _PUTIMAGE (kid_x, kid_y), kid&
```

Great. Now, we'll draw the Muscle Man. The Muscle Man will start running after the backpack, so you have to beat him! If you can't, then hit him with an apple like this (see Figure 6.2).

```
    'draw muscle man
    _PUTIMAGE (muscle_x, muscle_y), muscle&
    IF stunned > 0 THEN
        _PRINTSTRING (muscle_x + 25, muscle_y - 20), "OUCH!"
        stunned = stunned + 1
        IF stunned > 1000 THEN stunned = 0
    ELSE
        IF muscle_x < bp_x THEN
            muscle_x = muscle_x + 0.2
        ELSEIF muscle_x > bp_x THEN
            muscle_x = muscle_x - 0.2
        END IF
    END IF
```

Figure 6.2

*Beaming the
Muscle Man with
an apple stuns him.*

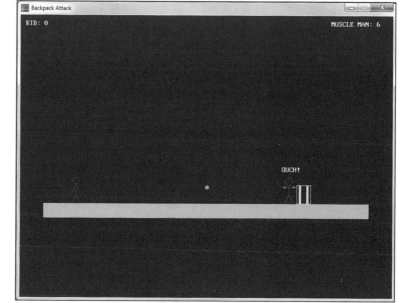

Next, we can draw the backpack and some stuff with it. Whenever the kid or Muscle Man gets the backpack, then they score a point! When that happens, the backpack goes to a new random location and falls down from the top of the screen again.

```
'draw backpack
bp_y = bp_y + 1
IF bp_y >= 360 THEN
    bp_y = 360
    'see if kid got it
    IF kid_x > bp_x AND kid_x < bp_x + 30 THEN
        bp_x = 50 + RND * 700
        bp_y = 0
        kid_score = kid_score + 1
    END IF
    'see if muscle man got it
    IF muscle_x > bp_x AND muscle_x < bp_x + 30 THEN
        bp_x = 50 + RND * 700
        bp_y = 0
        muscle_score = muscle_score + 1
    END IF
END IF
_PUTIMAGE (bp_x, bp_y), backpack&
```

Now for the apple throwing code. This is pretty fun to do in the game, so it demands an explanation! Okay, if you press the Z key, the apple is thrown left, while the X key throws the apple right. It will keep on going until it either hits the Muscle Man (and stuns him) or goes off the screen. You can only throw one apple at a time. And, sheesh, how many apples are you carrying? Must be from saving all the backpacks.

```
'draw the apple
IF throwing$ = "true" THEN
    apple_x = apple_x + apple_dir
    IF apple_x < 0 OR apple_x > 800 THEN throwing$ = "false"
    IF apple_x > muscle_x AND apple_x < muscle_x + 40 THEN
        throwing$ = "false"
        stunned = 1
    END IF
    _PUTIMAGE (apple_x, apple_y), apple&
END IF
```

The only time the game ends harshly (i.e., you lose!) is if you fall off the cliff. Yes, there's a cliff! As if this game wasn't already full of great features, there's a cliff! But be careful not to fall off! After that, the next two lines print out the score: Kid vs. Muscle Man. The screen shown in Figure 6.3 shows what happens if you fall off. The biggest problem with this, aside from dying, is Muscle Man will just keep stealing all the backpacks—forever and ever unless you end the game! See, that's not good.

```
IF gameover$ = "true" THEN
    _PRINTSTRING (350, 200), "G A M E   O V E R"
END IF

_PRINTSTRING (10, 10), "KID:" + STR$(kid_score)
_PRINTSTRING (670, 10), "MUSCLE MAN:" + STR$ (muscle_score)
```

Now, the last part of the game loop handles the keyboard input from the player. There are two keys for input (Left, Right), and two keys for shooting (Z, X), and then the Escape key to exit. At the very end, we call the END statement to end the game, but that's kind of unnecessary. SYSTEM is another way to end the game.

Figure 6.3

Don't fall off the edge of the world or you'll die!

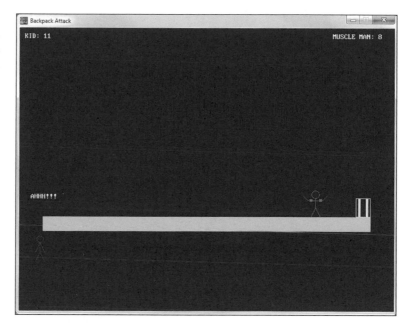

```
k$ = INKEY$
IF k$ <> "" THEN
    code = ASC(k$)
    IF code = 120 THEN 'x
        IF throwing$ = "false" THEN
            throwing$ = "true"
            apple_x = kid_x + 30
            apple_y = kid_y + 20
            apple_dir = 1
        END IF
    ELSEIF code = 122 THEN 'z
        IF throwing$ = "false" THEN
            throwing$ = "true"
            apple_x = kid_x + 30
            apple_y = kid_y + 20
            apple_dir = -1
        END IF
    ELSEIF code = 0 THEN 'special key
        code = ASC(k$, 2)
        IF code = 72 THEN 'up
        ELSEIF code = 80 THEN 'down
        ELSEIF code = 75 THEN 'left
            kid_x = kid_x - 4
        ELSEIF code = 77 THEN 'right
            kid_x = kid_x + 4
        END IF
```

```
          END IF
      END IF
      _DISPLAY
LOOP UNTIL k$ = CHR$(27)
END
```

 The game is found in the file called BackpackAttack.bas, if you prefer to load it rather than typing in the code (download files found at www.courseptr.com/downloads). You will learn a lot faster by typing in the code, but it's up to you.

Summary

This chapter featured one really big game with a lot of features, to give you more experience with a game loop, graphics, key input, and logic. One of the most important skills you now have is the ability to detect when two things hit each other in the game—like when the kid or Muscle Man gets the backpack. This is called *collision detection* and it's a very important skill to understand when programming games.

Quiz

Here is a little quiz to test whether you were paying attention. Try to answer the questions without looking up the answers first. This is not graded; it will just tell you whether you are ready to go to the next chapter or not. The answers are found in Appendix A.

1. What graphics command draws a line or a box?

A. LINE

B. DRAW_LINE

C. _LINE

D. DO_LINE

2. What command makes a new image that's used to draw shapes in the game?

A. IMG

B. IMAGE

C. _NEWIMAGE

D. NEW_IMAGE

3. What command draws an image to the screen?

A. DRAW

B. _PUTIMAGE

C. DRAW_IMAGE

D. PASTE

4. What command prints words like PRINT, but in graphics mode?

A. FANCY_PRINT

B. DRAW_WORDS

C. _PRINTSTRING

D. PRINT_STRING

5. What command draws a circle?

A. CIRCLE

B. _CIRCLE

C. DRAW_CIRCLE

D. CIRC

Homework

Your homework for this chapter is required to prove that you understand what you learned! If you have a hard time with this homework, then maybe you went too fast and might need to review the chapter again.

Instructions:

Using the new graphics commands you learned in this chapter, try to draw a portrait of yourself!

Chapter 7

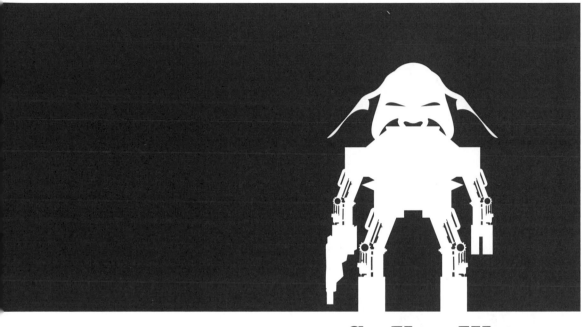

So You Wanna Be a Hero?

You have learned some really great things about programming video games in BASIC, especially in the previous chapter where you learned to make the most complete game. There are many helpful concepts in all of these games. Even if you don't understand every part of the BASIC code, you can see how things work in the game by studying it. I want you to be able to write your own game using these examples as a start, and make your own games that are way better than anything in this book.

So, we're going to make a new game that borrows ideas from the previous ones, and by doing so you will learn how similar the code is from one game to the next. Only the logic changes—that is, the code that makes things act a certain way, like Muscle Man chasing after the backpacks all by himself. That was game logic! In this chapter, you will learn a new programming ability to make complex games easier to make. Instead of a graphical game, we're going to make a Character Sheet Generator for a role-playing game (RPG).

More on Variables

You have been using variables in every program so far, possibly without really knowing their purpose. We have skipped over some of the code when making a game, because sometimes you can't explain every step; sometimes the best way to learn is to try things out on your own. For instance, we have to create a scrn& variable in most games, like so:

```
scrn& = _NEWIMAGE(800, 600, 32)
```

This line of code creates an image in memory that is 800×600 pixels—the size of the window. To create the game window:

```
SCREEN scrn&
```

Now, at this point, the window comes up and BASIC is ready to draw things in the game. You've been doing this for quite some time now and should be pretty familiar with it by now.

But, when we were moving the Kid or Muscle Man on the screen, there were a lot of these variables floating around, so to speak. One way to help organize our code a little better is by using custom data types, sometimes also called user-defined types.

A custom data type, or user-defined type, UDT, is a sort of object that contains several variables. By putting certain variables together in a UDT, it is easier to keep track of them. The way you create a UDT in BASIC is with the TYPE statement.

```
TYPE TypeName
    variables
END TYPE
```

So, let's say you want to keep track of your report card grades every semester. You could write a program using a TYPE like this one:

```
TYPE Grades
END TYPE
```

But, the question is, what do the variables look like inside the TYPE? You can't just create a number, like GPA (grade point average), without a data type included. Inside a custom TYPE, you have to define every variable specifically using the AS keyword. A keyword is a reserved word in BASIC. Here are the variable types we can use in a custom user-defined type in QB64 (see Table 7.1).

Table 7.1 BASIC Variable Data Types

Name	Description
INTEGER	Whole numbers from -32768 to 32767.
LONG	Whole numbers from -2,147,483,648 to 2,147,483,647.
SINGLE	Numbers with up to 7 decimal digits.
DOUBLE	Numbers with up to 15 decimal digits.
STRING	ASCII text characters

The most common variables you'll use will be INTEGER and STRING.

Gradebook

Now that you have the list of variable data types, you can fill in the Grades type with some variables. Let's start with the student name:

```
TYPE Grades
    Student AS STRING * 20
END TYPE
```

The definition of a STRING inside a TYPE has to include the length of the string. Just guess at how big of a word you will need to put into the variable, up to a maximum of 255. Next, let's add one subject. Depending on your teacher and your grade, you might get a letter grade (like A, B, C) or a number grade (like 100, 90, 80). We'll just use letter grades here. So, each subject will have to be a string. Because you can get an "A+" or "A-," then the string should be able to hold 2 characters. Here is a program that shows how to make your own gradebook.

```
_TITLE "Gradebook"
TYPE Gradebook
    Student AS STRING * 20
    Math AS STRING * 2
    Science AS STRING * 2
    Reading AS STRING * 2
    Writing AS STRING * 2
    Spelling AS STRING * 2
    Geography AS STRING * 2
    History AS STRING * 2
END TYPE

DIM grades AS Gradebook
grades.Student = "Bobby Fisher"
grades.Math = "A"
grades.Science = "B+"
grades.Reading = "C-"
grades.Writing = "A-"
grades.Spelling = "B-"
grades.Geography = "A+"
grades.History = "C+"

PRINT "Here are your grades:"
PRINT "Student: "; grades.Student
PRINT "Math: "; grades.Math
PRINT "Science: "; grades.Science
PRINT "Reading: "; grades.Reading
PRINT "Writing: "; grades.Writing
PRINT "Spelling: "; grades.Spelling
```

```
PRINT "Geography: "; grades.Geography
PRINT "History: "; grades.History
```

When you run this program, it should look like Figure 7.1.

Figure 7.1

The Gradebook program.

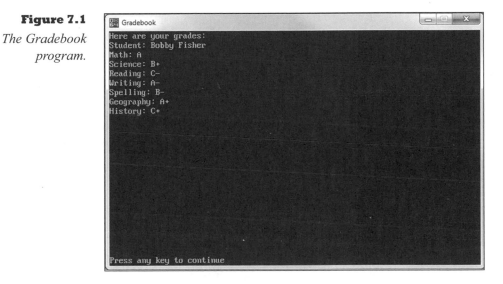

Character Generator

Next, we'll make a program that goes a little further. Have you ever played a role-playing game (RPG)? These are usually fantasy games, like *Lord of the Rings*, where you have a character who has skills and attributes and gains experience and levels up. It's the leveling up part that makes RPGs so much fun. We're going to make a Character Generator program, as a way to create a random RPG character. Let's begin. We need to use RANDOMIZE TIMER to start off RND using a different set of random numbers, so every time you run the program it will give you different random numbers.

```
_TITLE "Character Generator"
RANDOMIZE TIMER

TYPE Character
    Name AS STRING * 20
    Age AS INTEGER
    Race AS STRING * 20
    Class AS STRING * 20
    Specialty AS STRING * 20
    Strength AS INTEGER
    Dexterity AS INTEGER
```

111

```
      Willpower AS INTEGER
      Magic AS INTEGER
      Cunning AS INTEGER
      Constitution AS INTEGER
END TYPE
```

This is the TYPE for a Character, which can be re-used for many characters in the game. You could use this for heroes as well as monsters.

 These character attributes are borrowed from the game, *Dragon Age*, by BioWare/EA. You can change it to go with any game you want, like *Skyrim* or any other game.

Now, we can use this TYPE to create a new character with random attributes. You can change the Name, Race, Class, and Specialty to whatever you want; these are just examples.

```
DIM SHARED hero AS Character
hero.Name = "Gray Warden"
hero.Age = 20
hero.Race = "Human"
hero.Class = "Warrior"
hero.Specialty = "Champion"
hero.Strength = 5 + RND * 10
hero.Dexterity = 5 + RND * 10
hero.Willpower = 5 + RND * 10
hero.Magic = 5 + RND * 10
hero.Cunning = 5 + RND * 10
hero.Constitution = 5 + RND * 10
```

You could create a monster character too, by copying this code to make a new character with different attributes. Now let's work on printing out the character.

```
COLOR 14
PRINT "CHARACTER INFO"
COLOR 15
PRINT "Name: "; hero.Name
PRINT "Age: "; hero.Age
PRINT "Race: "; hero.Race
PRINT "Class: "; hero.Class
PRINT "Spec: "; hero.Specialty
```

```
PRINT "STR: "; hero.Strength
PRINT "DEX: "; hero.Dexterity
PRINT "WIL: "; hero.Willpower
PRINT "MAG: "; hero.Magic
PRINT "CUN: "; hero.Cunning
PRINT "CON: "; hero.Constitution
```

When you run the program at this point, it will look something like Figure 7.2.

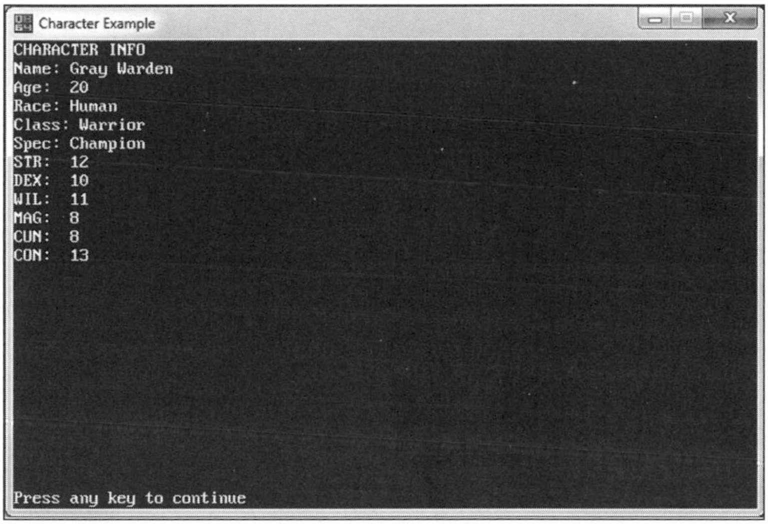

Figure 7.2

The Character Generator program.

```
CHARACTER INFO
Name: Gray Warden
Age:  20
Race: Human
Class: Warrior
Spec: Champion
STR:  12
DEX:  10
WIL:  11
MAG:  8
CUN:  8
CON:  13

Press any key to continue
```

Every time you run the program, the attributes will be different, allowing you to generate new characters.

A Better Character Generator

A more advanced character generator would also generate the race, class, and specialty from the attributes. So, let's add some logic to the generator and replace those typed-in values with new ones that are generated. This will be even more fun!

This new and improved version will do away with the *names* of the attributes like Race and Class, and instead use *numbers* to represent those things. This will make it easier to "roll the character." When we want to know the word that goes with one of these numbers, we can use a special function to print it out. Let's get started. First is the new Character type definition:

```
_TITLE "Character Generator"
RANDOMIZE TIMER

TYPE Character
    Name AS STRING * 20
    Age AS INTEGER
    Race AS INTEGER
    Class AS INTEGER
    Specialty AS INTEGER
    Strength AS INTEGER
    Dexterity AS INTEGER
    Willpower AS INTEGER
    Magic AS INTEGER
    Cunning AS INTEGER
    Constitution AS INTEGER
END TYPE
```

Here is the code that generates or "rolls" the character, as RPG fans are fond of calling the process. For a tabletop "pencil & paper" game with miniatures, players will usually roll these basic attributes and then a whole bunch more for their new character's skills and abilities.

```
PRINT "Creating character..."
DIM SHARED hero AS Character
hero.Name = "Gray Warden"
hero.Age = 20
hero.Strength = 5 + RND * 10
hero.Dexterity = 5 + RND * 10
hero.Willpower = 5 + RND * 10
hero.Magic = 5 + RND * 10
hero.Cunning = 5 + RND * 10
hero.Constitution = 5 + RND * 10

PRINT "Generating the race..."
hero.Race = INT(RND * 3)

PRINT "Generating the class..."
IF hero.Dexterity > 10 OR hero.Cunning > 10 THEN
    hero.Class = 0 'rogue
ELSEIF hero.Magic > 10 OR hero.Willpower > 10 THEN
    hero.Class = 1 'mage
ELSE
    hero.Class = 2 'warrior
END IF

PRINT "Generating the specialty..."
hero.Specialty = INT(RND * 4)
```

Once the character has been "rolled," we can print out the character's information all at once.

```
COLOR 14
PRINT
PRINT "CHARACTER INFO"
COLOR 15
PRINT "Name: "; hero.Name
PRINT "Age: "; hero.Age
PRINT "Race: "; GetRace(hero.Race)
PRINT "Class: "; GetClass(hero.Class)
PRINT "Spec: "; GetSpecialty(hero.Class, hero.Specialty)
PRINT "STR: "; hero.Strength
PRINT "DEX: "; hero.Dexterity
PRINT "WIL: "; hero.Willpower
PRINT "MAG: "; hero.Magic
PRINT "CUN: "; hero.Cunning
PRINT "CON: "; hero.Constitution
END
```

The GetRace() function expects to receive a number parameter, and returns either Human, Elf, or Dwarf.

```
FUNCTION GetRace$ (n)
IF n = 0 THEN
    GetRace$ = "Human"
ELSEIF n = 1 THEN
    GetRace$ = "Elf"
ELSEIF n = 2 THEN
    GetRace$ = "Dwarf"
END IF
END FUNCTION
```

The GetClass() function expects to receive one of three numbers as a parameter (n), and returns the class name of either Rogue, Mage, or Warrior.

```
FUNCTION GetClass$ (n)
IF n = 0 THEN
    GetClass$ = "Rogue"
ELSEIF n = 1 THEN
    GetClass$ = "Mage"
ELSEIF n = 2 THEN
    GetClass$ = "Warrior"
END IF
END FUNCTION
```

The GetSpecialty() function is used any time you want to print out the character's specialty. By passing the race and specialty numbers, this function figures out which specialty name to return. This is not the *best* way to return a string, but it is the *simplest* way. If you want to change the names of any of these specialties to make a character around *your* favorite game, go ahead and change the names!

```
FUNCTION GetSpecialty$ (class, spec)
IF class = 0 THEN
    IF spec = 0 THEN
        GetSpecialty = "Assassin"
    ELSEIF spec = 1 THEN
        GetSpecialty = "Bard"
    ELSEIF spec = 2 THEN
        GetSpecialty = "Duelist"
    ELSE
        GetSpecialty = "Ranger"
    END IF
ELSEIF class = 1 THEN
    IF spec = 0 THEN
        GetSpecialty = "Arcane Warrior"
    ELSEIF spec = 1 THEN
        GetSpecialty = "Shapeshifter"
    ELSEIF spec = 2 THEN
        GetSpecialty = "Spirit Healer"
    ELSE
        GetSpecialty = "Blood Mage"
    END IF
ELSEIF class = 2 THEN
    IF spec = 0 THEN
        GetSpecialty = "Berserker"
    ELSEIF spec = 1 THEN
        GetSpecialty = "Champion"
    ELSEIF spec = 2 THEN
        GetSpecialty = "Reaver"
    ELSEIF spec = 3 THEN
        GetSpecialty = "Templar"
    END IF
END IF
END FUNCTION
```

Now, go ahead and run the program. You will want to run it over and over again a few times to see what types of characters you can generate. In Figure 7.3, we have a Warrior Champion character that has been generated. This is one of the four Warrior specialties; the other three are Berserker, Reaver, and Templar.

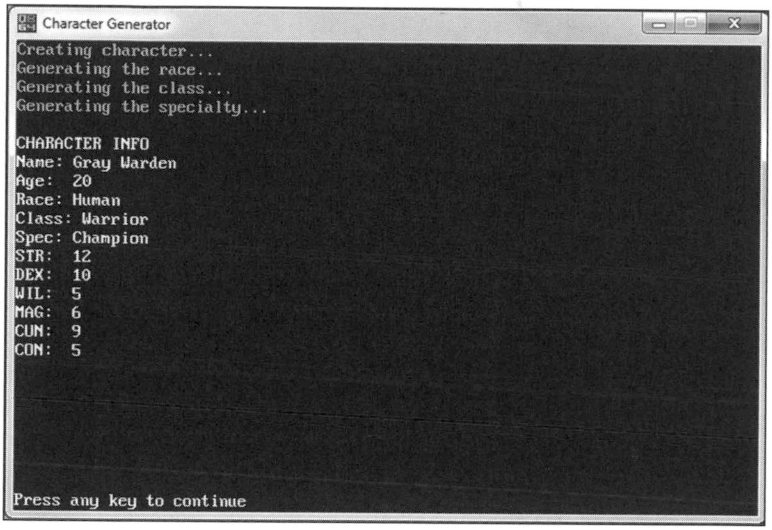

Figure 7.3

Rolling a Warrior Champion character.

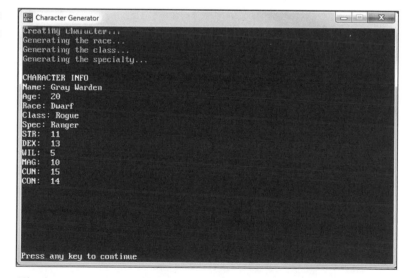

Next, in Figure 7.4, is an example of a Rogue Ranger. The other three Rogue specialties that might come up are `Assassin`, `Bard`, and `Duelist`.

Figure 7.4

Rolling a Rogue Ranger character.

The last example in Figure 7.5 shows a Mage/Arcane Warrior that came up in this character roll. The other types of Mage specialties are `Shapeshifter`, `Spirit Healer`, and `Blood Mage`.

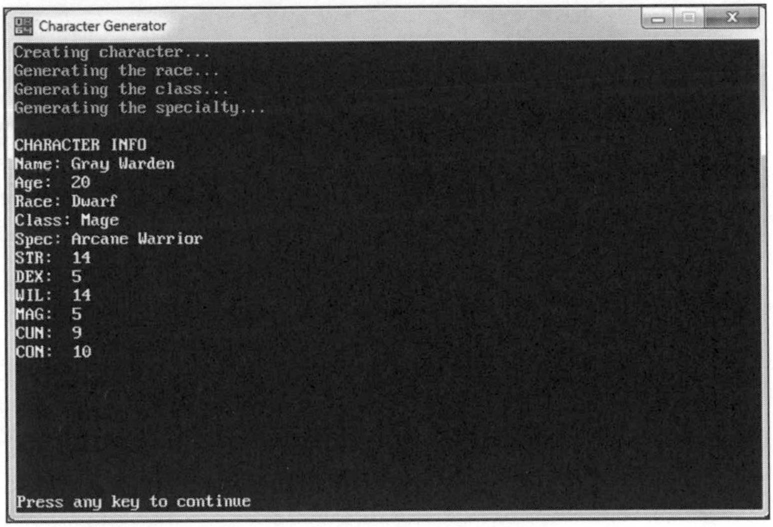

Figure 7.5

*Rolling a Mage
Arcane Warrior
character.*

```
Character Generator                                              _ □ X
Creating character...
Generating the race...
Generating the class...
Generating the specialty...

CHARACTER INFO
Name: Gray Warden
Age:  20
Race: Dwarf
Class: Mage
Spec: Arcane Warrior
STR:  14
DEX:  5
WIL:  14
MAG:  5
CUN:  9
CON:  10




Press any key to continue
```

Summary

This is just the beginning of a basic character generator. If we
wanted to really make it more complete, then we could add skills
and abilities as well, depending on the class and specialty. But,
this is a good example for now, and you gained some good experience working with custom types!

Quiz

Here is a little quiz to test whether you were paying attention. Try
to answer the questions without looking up the answers first. This
is not graded; it will just tell you whether you are ready to move
on to the next chapter. The answers are found in Appendix A.

1. What statement do you use to make your own custom container for variables?

A. TYPE

B. CONTAINER

C. BACKPACK

D. LOCKER

2. What type of variable is most often used for numbers?

A. STRING

B. BYTE

C. INTEGER

D. DIM

3. What BASIC statement is used for thinking?

A. IF

B. DIM

C. DO

D. FOR

4. What type of variable does FUNCTION GetRace$ (n) return?

A. INTEGER

B. DOUBLE

C. LONG

D. STRING

5. What statement should you call before using RND to roll random numbers like dice?

A. END

B. CLS

C. RANDOMIZE

D. SCREEN

Homework

Your homework for this chapter is required to prove that you understand what you learned! If you have a hard time with this homework, then maybe you went too fast and might need to review the chapter again.

Instructions:

Using the Character Generator as an example, make your own character generator program for your favorite RPG—it can be any game you want!

Chapter 8

Super Squirt Gun
Laser Bazooka

T here comes a time when diplomacy has failed and you can't help but go to war. Such is the case when your brother or sister shoots you with a squirt gun. At times like this, it's time to get out the heavy artillery—water balloons or a super soaker!

In this chapter you will learn to make a real-time arcade-style shooting game similar to the old Atari "Air Sea Battle" game from many years ago. This chapter shows you how to create the game step by step, explaining each step along the way. Study each step carefully so you will learn how to make the game, one piece at a time. I think that's the best way to learn!

Setting Up the Game

The first thing you'll need to do is write the code for the game loop. As you have seen in other examples, we always do this with DO and LOOP.

This game is organized in a special way. Can you tell how it looks different from the last game?

The DO and LOOP statements have only one line between them, a CALL Update. This is all there is to the loop! Don't you think it is easier to understand the source code this way? This is called a *structured* program. Instead of just writing code straight away, we are dividing it up.

SECRET

Type this code in to a new program file in QB64. Save the file as SuperGame.bas. Or, you can load the finished game into QB64 and just run it. But where's the fun in that? It's better to build the game step by step in order to learn to be a game programmer.

```
_TITLE "Super Squirt Gun Laser Bazooka"
DIM SHARED k$
CALL Load
DO
    CALL Update
LOOP
END
```

```
SUB Load ()
scrn& = _NEWIMAGE(800, 600, 32)
SCREEN scrn&
END SUB

SUB Update ()
k$ = INKEY$
IF k$ = CHR$(27) THEN END
END SUB
```

 There are two SUBs in this game, called Load and Update.

If you run the program now, you will see a blank window come up. That's a good start, but let's at least get the background graphics to show up, just for starters.

Adding the Background

To add the background to the game, we need to create a shared variable called bg&, which stands for "background." It has been added here in bold:

```
_TITLE "Super Squirt Gun Laser Bazooka"
DIM SHARED k$, bg&
```

 The bg& variable keeps track of the background image.

There are no changes to the next part of the program:

```
CALL Load
DO
    CALL Update
LOOP
END
```

Now, in the Load sub-procedure, this is where we want to create the graphics for the game. The background will be an ocean scene with a sky. In the game, you will control a submarine at the bottom of the ocean. There will be enemy ships and other subs cruising along above, and you must shoot them with torpedoes. But there's a catch: this will be the first game where the computer objects shoot back! Add the new part shown. Be sure to add the final line that calls _DEST scrn&, which is very important! Otherwise, nothing will show up because all drawings will keep going to the background.

```
SUB Load ()
scrn& = _NEWIMAGE(800, 600, 32)
SCREEN scrn&

'make background
bg& = _NEWIMAGE(800, 600, 32)
_DEST bg&
blue1& = _RGB(100, 100, 255)
blue2& = _RGB(40, 40, 220)
blue3& = _RGB(40, 40, 180)
LINE (0, 0)-(799, 100), blue1&, BF
LINE (0, 101)-(799, 300), blue2&, BF
LINE (0, 301)-(799, 599), blue3&, BF
_DEST scrn&
END SUB
```

Always make sure _DEST scrn& comes at the very end of the Load() sub-procedure. Otherwise, when the game starts, nothing will show up on the screen!

Now, as for the Update sub-procedure, there is just one new line that draws the background, and one more line that calls _DISPLAY. After making this final change, go ahead and run the program by pressing F5. You should see the screen shown in Figure 8.1.

```
SUB Update ()
_PUTIMAGE (0, 0), bg&
_DISPLAY
k$ = INKEY$
IF k$ = CHR$(27) THEN END
END SUB
```

Figure 8.1

We have a background!

Adding the Ship

Now that we have a sky and ocean, let's add a ship that will float on the ocean. Better yet, a ship that moves! First, add the new variables as shown for the new ship object.

```
_TITLE "Super Squirt Gun Laser Bazooka"
DIM SHARED k$, bg&, ship&, ship_x, ship_y
```

The ship& variable contains the image of the ship.

Now we can build the ship in the Load() sub-procedure. Make the changes shown. Most importantly, make sure _DEST scrn& is still at the end. After the game's graphics are made, this statement causes BASIC to draw to the screen again.

```
SUB Load ()
scrn& = _NEWIMAGE(800, 600, 32)
SCREEN scrn&
```

```
'make background
bg& = _NEWIMAGE(800, 600, 32)
_DEST bg&
blue1& = _RGB(100, 100, 255)
blue2& = _RGB(40, 40, 220)
blue3& = _RGB(40, 40, 180)
LINE (0, 0)-(799, 100), blue1&, BF
LINE (0, 101)-(799, 300), blue2&, BF
LINE (0, 301)-(799, 599), blue3&, BF

'make a ship
ship& = _NEWIMAGE(60, 60, 32)
_DEST ship&
tanned& = _RGB(180, 180, 0)
brown& = _RGB(150, 150, 0)
dkbrown& = _RGB(100, 100, 0)
LINE (0, 30)-(59, 30), tanned&
LINE (0, 30)-(15, 45), tanned&
LINE (15, 45)-(45, 45), tanned&
LINE (45, 45)-(59, 30), tanned&
PAINT (30, 40), tanned&
LINE (10, 25)-(50, 30), brown&, BF
LINE (20, 20)-(40, 25), dkbrown&, BF
LINE (15, 25)-(5, 20), dkbrown&
LINE (45, 25)-(55, 20), dkbrown&
ship_x = 800
ship_y = 60
_DEST scrn&
END SUB
```

Now, time to draw and move the ship! Here are the changes you need to make to the Update() sub-procedure:

```
SUB Update ()
_PUTIMAGE (0, 0), bg&
_PUTIMAGE (ship_x, ship_y), ship&
_DISPLAY

'move the ship
ship_x = ship_x - 0.5
IF ship_x < -60 THEN ship_x = 800

k$ = INKEY$
IF k$ = CHR$(27) THEN END
END SUB
```

That's it for the ship! Go ahead and run the program. It should look like Figure 8.2.

Figure 8.2

A ship is moving across the water.

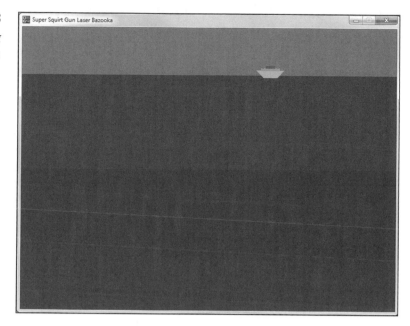

Adding the Subs

Now you are ready to add the enemy submarines that will move under the water. They will move a bit slower than the ship because they're underwater. The great thing about using an image for our graphics is, once you make the ship or submarine, you can draw it twice to make two! The only time the game "draws" the graphics is in the Load() sub-procedure. After that is done, it's the image that gets drawn when you're playing the game. Drawing an image is really fast, while drawing lines and other shapes is slow. That's why we draw the shapes first and only once when the game is starting up.

First, you will need to add the new submarine variables at the top of the program. Here is the new code in bold. Do you see that there are two variables for the submarine's x and y position? We have sub1_x, sub1_y, and sub2_x, sub2_y. This is all you need to add a second sub!

```
_TITLE "Super Squirt Gun Laser Bazooka"
DIM SHARED k$, bg&, ship&, ship_x, ship_y
DIM SHARED submarine&, sub1_x, sub1_y, sub2_x, sub2_y
```

The submarine& variable contains the submarine image.

Now you can add the new code in the Load() sub-procedure to make the submarine. The new part is highlighted in bold. Just ignore the code you have already typed in, and add the bold part. The whole SUB Load () is being shown again so you know where to add the code.

```
SUB Load ()
scrn& = _NEWIMAGE(800, 600, 32)
SCREEN scrn&

'make background
bg& = _NEWIMAGE(800, 600, 32)
_DEST bg&
blue1& = _RGB(100, 100, 255)
blue2& = _RGB(40, 40, 220)
blue3& = _RGB(40, 40, 180)
LINE (0, 0)-(799, 100), blue1&, BF
LINE (0, 101)-(799, 300), blue2&, BF
LINE (0, 301)-(799, 599), blue3&, BF

'make a ship
ship& = _NEWIMAGE(60, 60, 32)
_DEST ship&
tanned& = _RGB(180, 180, 0)
brown& = _RGB(150, 150, 0)
dkbrown& = _RGB(100, 100, 0)
LINE (0, 30)-(59, 30), tanned&
LINE (0, 30)-(15, 45), tanned&
LINE (15, 45)-(45, 45), tanned&
LINE (45, 45)-(59, 30), tanned&
PAINT (30, 40), tanned&
LINE (10, 25)-(50, 30), brown&, BF
LINE (20, 20)-(40, 25), dkbrown&, BF
LINE (15, 25)-(5, 20), dkbrown&
LINE (45, 25)-(55, 20), dkbrown&
ship_x = 800
ship_y = 60

'make a sub
submarine& = _NEWIMAGE(60, 60, 32)
_DEST submarine&
```

```
yellow& = _RGB(220, 220, 20)
LINE (0, 28)-(59, 32), yellow&, BF
LINE (58, 25)-(59, 35), yellow&, BF
LINE (3, 27)-(54, 33), yellow&, BF
LINE (7, 26)-(47, 34), yellow&, BF
LINE (15, 24)-(40, 35), yellow&, BF
LINE (28, 20)-(32, 24), yellow&, BF
LINE (30, 13)-(30, 20), yellow&, BF
LINE (28, 13)-(30, 13), yellow&, BF
sub1_x = 500
sub1_y = 160
sub2_x = 200
sub2_y = 300

_DEST scrn&
END SUB
```

Great! Now for moving and drawing the two subs. For that, we'll have to add some new code to SUB Update () again. There's a part near the top that draws the two subs, and a part later that moves the subs. Be sure to add both parts of new code.

```
SUB Update ()
_PUTIMAGE (0, 0), bg&
_PUTIMAGE (ship_x, ship_y), ship&
_PUTIMAGE (sub1_x, sub1_y), submarino&
_PUTIMAGE (sub2_x, sub2_y), submarine&
_DISPLAY

'move the ship
ship_x = ship_x - 0.5
IF ship_x < -60 THEN ship_x = 800

'move the subs
sub1_x = sub1_x - 0.4
IF sub1_x < -60 THEN sub1_x = 800
sub2_x = sub2_x - 0.3
IF sub2_x < -60 THEN sub2_x = 800

k$ = INKEY$
IF k$ = CHR$(27) THEN END
END SUB
```

Now go ahead and run the game. You should see the screen shown in Figure 8.3.

That's it for the ship! Run the program. Woohoo! We have a ship and submarines, and they're moving, and they re-spawn at the other side when they get to the edge of the screen. This is some good progress!

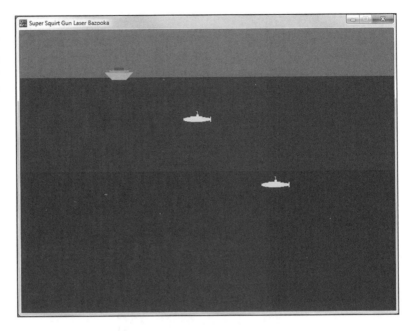

Adding the Player's Gun

The player needs something to play with against the enemy ship and subs. We could let the player have a submarine and fight against the enemies. That would be fun! But, maybe next time. The game was set up so you have to shoot at the enemy ships from the bottom. So, we have to add a gun at the bottom and let the player shoot it. This is a simple game where you can only shoot up, not at an angle. So, you have to time your shots so they will hit a ship, and there's no aiming.

First, you can add the new variables to the top:

```
_TITLE "Super Squirt Gun Laser Bazooka"
DIM SHARED k$, bg&, ship&, ship_x, ship_y
DIM SHARED submarine&, sub1_x, sub1_y, sub2_x, sub2_y
DIM SHARED player&, player_x, player_y
```

The player& variable contains the image of the player's gun at the bottom of the screen.

Next, add the code to Load() to make the gun:

```
SUB Load ()
scrn& = _NEWIMAGE(800, 600, 32)
SCREEN scrn&

'make background
bg& = _NEWIMAGE(800, 600, 32)
_DEST bg&
blue1& = _RGB(100, 100, 255)
blue2& = _RGB(40, 40, 220)
blue3& = _RGB(40, 40, 180)
LINE (0, 0)-(799, 100), blue1&, BF
LINE (0, 101)-(799, 300), blue2&, BF
LINE (0, 301)-(799, 599), blue3&, BF

'make a ship
ship& = _NEWIMAGE(60, 60, 32)
_DEST ship&
tanned& = _RGB(180, 180, 0)
brown& = _RGB(150, 150, 0)
dkbrown& = _RGB(100, 100, 0)
LINE (0, 30)-(59, 30), tanned&
LINE (0, 30)-(15, 45), tanned&
LINE (15, 45)-(45, 45), tanned&
LINE (45, 45)-(59, 30), tanned&
PAINT (30, 40), tanned&
LINE (10, 25)-(50, 30), brown&, BF
LINE (20, 20)-(40, 25), dkbrown&, BF
LINE (15, 25)-(5, 20), dkbrown&
LINE (45, 25)-(55, 20), dkbrown&
ship_x = 800
ship_y = 60

'make a sub
submarine& = _NEWIMAGE(60, 60, 32)
_DEST submarine&
yellow& = _RGB(220, 220, 20)
LINE (0, 28)-(59, 32), yellow&, BF
LINE (58, 25)-(59, 35), yellow&, BF
LINE (3, 27)-(54, 33), yellow&, BF
```

```
LINE (7, 26)-(47, 34), yellow&, BF
LINE (15, 24)-(40, 35), yellow&, BF
LINE (28, 20)-(32, 24), yellow&, BF
LINE (30, 13)-(30, 20), yellow&, BF
LINE (28, 13)-(30, 13), yellow&, BF
sub1_x = 500
sub1_y = 160
sub2_x = 200
sub2_y = 300

'make the player's gun
player& = _NEWIMAGE(60, 60, 32)
_DEST player&
white& = _RGB(255, 255, 255)
LINE (10, 40)-(50, 59), white&, BF
LINE (20, 30)-(40, 40), white&, BF
LINE (29, 15)-(31, 30), white&, BF
player_x = 370
player_y = 535

_DEST scrn&
END SUB
```

Alrighty then! Next—you guessed it!—you have to draw it. Since the player's gun doesn't move, this is a cinch:

```
SUB Update ()
_PUTIMAGE (0, 0), bg&
_PUTIMAGE (ship_x, ship_y), ship&
_PUTIMAGE (sub1_x, sub1_y), submarine&
_PUTIMAGE (sub2_x, sub2_y), submarine&
_PUTIMAGE (player_x, player_y), player&
_DISPLAY

'move the ship
ship_x = ship_x - 0.5
IF ship_x < -60 THEN ship_x = 800

'move the subs
sub1_x = sub1_x - 0.4
IF sub1_x < -60 THEN sub1_x = 800
sub2_x = sub2_x - 0.3
IF sub2_x < -60 THEN sub2_x = 800

k$ = INKEY$
IF k$ = CHR$(27) THEN END
END SUB
```

Go ahead and run the game now after this change. You should now see the player's gun at the bottom like in Figure 8.4.

Figure 8.4

The player's gun has been added.

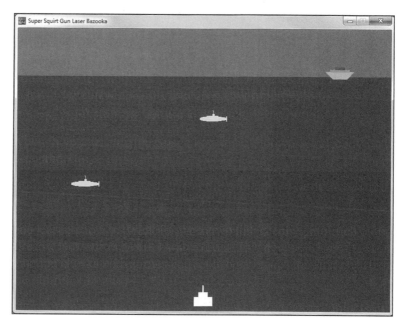

Shooting

Now you will make it so the player can shoot at the enemy ships! This will be really fun.

To shoot from the player's gun, we don't need an image—just three variables:

* shooting—A number that = 1 when shooting, or 0 when not.
* shot_x—A number for the X position of the bullet.
* shot_y—A number for the Y position of the bullet.

When the player hits the Space key, if a bullet wasn't already just fired, then three things happen.

First, we set shooting = 1, to tell the game that a bullet was fired from the player's gun.

Second, set shot_x and shot_y equal to the starting position of the shot. This position will be right in front of the gun.

Then, as the game runs, when it sees that `shooting = 1`, then it will move the bullet up the screen!

Isn't it interesting how you don't just draw the bullet going up, but you have to set things up for later? That's a very important trick to game programming that you should remember! You don't have to do things instantly when they happen. It's better to set a *flag* (like the `shooting` variable) that causes something to happen, rather than making it happen all of a sudden.

Think of it like this: when the lunch bell rings, do you instantly teleport to the lunch room? No! It just tells you, "Hey, it's time for lunch!" Only then do you start putting away your school work and begin waiting for the teacher to dismiss you for lunch. You don't get to just instantly start eating.

That's what it's like when you fire a bullet in the game. It's like telling the game, "Hey, shoot!" When this happens, the game puts the bullet in the right spot (like getting in line for lunch), and then begins moving the bullet up the screen (like getting your lunch and sitting down to eat). These things happen in steps, not all at the same time, and not instantly.

Okay, now that you understand how it works, let's write the code! Add this to the top of the program:

```
DIM SHARED shot_x, shot_y, shooting
shooting = 0
```

You don't have to do anything in `Load()` this time, because you just draw a small square for the bullet, not an image.

All the real work for shooting is in the `Update()` sub-procedure. Let's take a look at the changes. Do you see the first part starting with `IF shooting = 1 THEN`? That's where the game checks to see if it's time to shoot, if the player hit the Space key. If that happens, it goes, "Woohoo, time to shoot!" Then, the little red box is drawn, and this is the bullet. Also, if the bullet goes off the top of the screen, then shooting is turned off (`shooting = 0`).

 There's no image for bullets! The game just draws a little red box for the bullet. It probably would be nicer to draw a torpedo in this game since we're fighting against enemy ships and subs in the ocean. How about we pretend the little red box is a *photon* torpedo? Hey, it's your game, you can call it anything you want!

```
SUB Update ()
_PUTIMAGE (0, 0), bg&
_PUTIMAGE (ship_x, ship_y), ship&
_PUTIMAGE (sub1_x, sub1_y), submarine&
_PUTIMAGE (sub2_x, sub2_y), submarine&
_PUTIMAGE (player_x, player_y), player&
IF shooting = 1 THEN
    red& = _RGB(255, 0, 0)
    LINE (shot_x - 2, shot_y - 2)-(shot_x + 2, shot_y +
2), red&, BF
    shot_y = shot_y - 1.0
    IF shot_y < 0 THEN shooting = 0
END IF
_DISPLAY

'move the ship
ship_x = ship_x - 0.5
IF ship_x < -60 THEN ship_x = 800

'move the subs
sub1_x = sub1_x - 0.4
IF sub1_x < -60 THEN sub1_x = 800
sub2_x = sub2_x - 0.3
IF sub2_x < -60 THEN sub2_x = 800

k$ = INKEY$
IF k$ = CHR$(27) THEN END
IF k$ = CHR$(32) AND shooting = 0 THEN
    shooting = 1
    shot_x = 400
    shot_y = 550
END IF
END SUB
```

Go ahead and run the game now after this change. When you press Space, it should fire a bullet as shown in Figure 8.5. Look carefully. The bullet is a small dot just above the gun.

Figure 8.5

Shooting at the enemy ships.

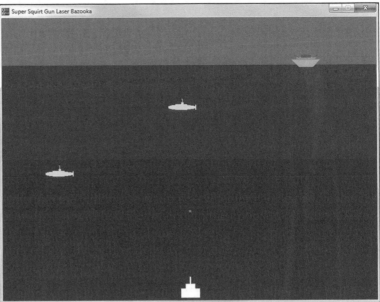

Blowing Stuff Up!

A-ha, now we can fire at the enemy ships, but nothing happens when you hit them! So, it's time to add the part to the game where you can blow them up!

In video game programming, hitting enemies with a bullet is tricky. You can use a special trick called *collision detection*. Get it? A collision is when something crashes. Detection is when you see it, like detecting an enemy jet on RADAR. When that happens, it's time to fire the anti-aircraft guns! Hey, that sounds like it would make a sweet game too!

Collision detection is a trick where you *pretend* that two objects hit each other in a game. It's 100% up to you (the programmer) to decide what happens. You can even ignore some hits if you want, and pay attention to others. Like, in some games, it's okay to hit your friend with your bullets, but they still destroy the enemy.

I was playing *Dragon Age: Origins*, and used a fire bomb to attack a group of enemy guys, and the bomb didn't hurt any of my own team at all! That's kind of fake, but it makes the game more fun. It would be a real pain if you had to worry about hitting your own guys.

Making an explosion look real is difficult unless you have an artist make a realistic looking explosion image. But, we don't have an artist, and we have to draw our graphics with BASIC. So, let's just do a simple filled circle and draw it over an enemy ship when we blow it up.

First, add this to the top:

```
DIM SHARED boom&, booming, boom_x, boom_y
booming = 0
```

The boom& variable contains the image of the explosion (just a red circle).

Next, add this code to the Load() sub-procedure:

```
'make explosion
boom& = _NEWIMAGE(60, 60, 32)
_DEST boom&
red& = _RGB(255, 0, 0)
CIRCLE (30, 30), 28, red&
PAINT (30, 30), red&
```

Next, add this to the Update() sub-procedure, toward the bottom but before the k$ = inkey$ line. This is the code to check for collisions between the bullet and the three enemy ships.

```
'look for a collision
IF shooting = 1 THEN
    'hit the ship?
    IF shot_x > ship_x AND shot_x < ship_x + 60 THEN
        IF shot_y > ship_y AND shot_y < ship_y + 60 THEN
            shooting = 0
            booming = 1
            boom_x = ship_x
            boom_y = ship_y
            ship_x = 800
        END IF
    END IF
```

```
    'hit sub1?
    IF shot_x > sub1_x AND shot_x < sub1_x + 60 THEN
        IF shot_y > sub1_y AND shot_y < sub1_y + 60 THEN
            shooting = 0
            booming = 1
            boom_x - sub1_x
            boom_y = sub1_y
            sub1_x = 800
        END IF
    END IF

    'hit sub2?
    IF shot_x > sub2_x AND shot_x < sub2_x + 60 THEN
        IF shot_x > sub2_y AND shot_y < sub2_y + 60 THEN
            shooting = 0
            booming = 1
            boom_x = sub2_x
            boom_y = sub2_y
            sub2_x = 800
        END IF
    END IF
END IF
```

Right after that, add this code also, which draws the explosion if there's a hit.

```
'explosion time?
IF booming = 1 THEN
    _PUTIMAGE (boom_x, boom_y), boom&
    _DISPLAY
    SLEEP 1 'pause for 1 second
    booming = 0
END IF
```

When you run the game at this point, you should be able to shoot at the enemy ships and blow them up! See Figure 8.6. If you're having any problems with putting the new code in the right place, don't worry—the entire game is shown at the end of the chapter for reference.

Figure 8.6

We have a direct hit! Enemy submarine destroyed!

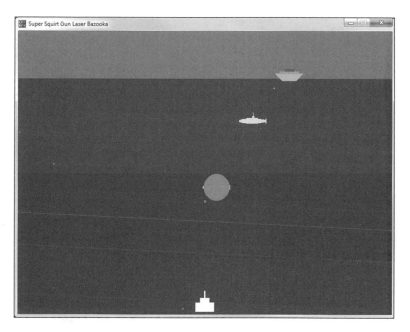

Keeping Score

There's just one more thing we need to do to finish the game: keep track of score. This will be pretty easy.

First, add this new variable near the top:

```
DIM SHARED score
score = 0
```

You score a point when an enemy ship is destroyed. You can add the line to the code that does the explosion.

```
'explosion time?
IF booming = 1 THEN
    _PUTIMAGE (boom_x, boom_y), boom&
    _DISPLAY
    SLEEP 1
    booming = 0
    score = score + 1
END IF
```

Finally, the score is printed out. Add these two lines just before the _DISPLAY line in Update(). If you aren't sure where it goes, check the entire program listing below.

```
_PRINTMODE _KEEPBACKGROUND
_PRINTSTRING (0, 0), STR$(score)
```

Go ahead and run the game again. The score is printed in the upper-left corner of the window (Figure 8.7). That's it! We're done!

Figure 8.7

The score is shown in the upper-left corner.

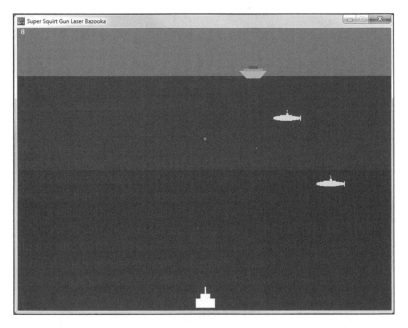

 SECRET The ship at the top is really hard to hit! Maybe it should be worth two points? If you want to give the player more points for hitting the ship, you could add to the score in the collision code where the bullet hits the ship.

The Complete Game

This was a pretty big game, because so much is happening at once! Building a game from scratch like this, step by step, takes a lot of concentration! Here is the complete game without any breaks. Sometimes source code goes together like a puzzle and only works if the parts are in the right places.

```
_TITLE "Super Squirt Gun Laser Bazooka"
DIM SHARED k$, bg&, ship&, ship_x, ship_y
DIM SHARED submarine&, sub1_x, sub1_y, sub2_x, sub2_y
DIM SHARED player&, player_x, player_y
DIM SHARED shot_x, shot_y, shooting
shooting = 0
DIM SHARED boom&, booming, boom_x, boom_y
booming = 0
DIM SHARED score
score = 0

CALL Load
DO
    CALL Update
LOOP
END

SUB Load ()
scrn& = _NEWIMAGE(800, 600, 32)
SCREEN scrn&

'make background
bg& = _NEWIMAGE(800, 600, 32)
_DEST bg&
blue1& = _RGB(100, 100, 255)
blue2& = _RGB(40, 40, 220)
blue3& = _RGB(40, 40, 180)
LINE (0, 0)-(799, 100), blue1&, BF
LINE (0, 101)-(799, 300), blue2&, BF
LINE (0, 301)-(799, 599), blue3&, BF

'make a ship
ship& = _NEWIMAGE(60, 60, 32)
_DEST ship&
tanned& = _RGB(180, 180, 0)
brown& = _RGB(150, 150, 0)
dkbrown& = _RGB(100, 100, 0)
LINE (0, 30)-(59, 30), tanned&
LINE (0, 30)-(15, 45), tanned&
LINE (15, 45)-(45, 45), tanned&
LINE (45, 45)-(59, 30), tanned&
PAINT (30, 40), tanned&
LINE (10, 25)-(50, 30), brown&, BF
LINE (20, 20)-(40, 25), dkbrown&, BF
LINE (15, 25)-(5, 20), dkbrown&
LINE (45, 25)-(55, 20), dkbrown&
ship_x = 800
ship_y = 60
```

```
'make a sub
submarine& = _NEWIMAGE(60, 60, 32)
_DEST submarine&
yellow& = _RGB(220, 220, 20)
LINE (0, 28)-(59, 32), yellow&, BF
LINE (58, 25)-(59, 35), yellow&, BF
LINE (3, 27)-(54, 33), yellow&, BF
LINE (7, 26)-(47, 34), yellow&, BF
LINE (15, 24)-(40, 35), yellow&, BF
LINE (28, 20)-(32, 24), yellow&, BF
LINE (30, 13)-(30, 20), yellow&, BF
LINE (28, 13)-(30, 13), yellow&, BF
sub1_x = 500
sub1_y = 160
sub2_x = 200
sub2_y = 300

'make the player's gun
player& = _NEWIMAGE(60, 60, 32)
_DEST player&
white& = _RGB(255, 255, 255)
LINE (10, 40)-(50, 59), white&, BF
LINE (20, 30)-(40, 40), white&, BF
LINE (29, 15)-(31, 30), white&, BF
player_x = 370
player_y = 535

'make explosion
boom& = _NEWIMAGE(60, 60, 32)
_DEST boom&
red& = _RGB(255, 0, 0)
CIRCLE (30, 30), 28, red&
PAINT (30, 30), red&

_DEST scrn&
END SUB

SUB Update ()
_PUTIMAGE (0, 0), bg&
_PUTIMAGE (ship_x, ship_y), ship&
_PUTIMAGE (sub1_x, sub1_y), submarine&
_PUTIMAGE (sub2_x, sub2_y), submarine&
_PUTIMAGE (player_x, player_y), player&
IF shooting = 1 THEN
    red& = _RGB(255, 0, 0)
    LINE (shot_x - 2, shot_y - 2)-(shot_x + 2, shot_y ↵
+ 2), red&, BF
    shot_y = shot_y - 1.0
```

```
        IF shot_y < 0 THEN shooting = 0
    END IF
    _PRINTMODE _KEEPBACKGROUND
    _PRINTSTRING (0, 0), STR$(score)
    _DISPLAY

    'move the ship
    ship_x = ship_x - 0.5
    IF ship_x < -60 THEN ship_x = 800

    'move the subs
    sub1_x = sub1_x - 0.4
    IF sub1_x < -60 THEN sub1_x = 800
    sub2_x = sub2_x - 0.3
    IF sub2_x < -60 THEN sub2_x = 800

    'look for a collision
    IF shooting = 1 THEN
        'hit the ship?
        IF shot_x > ship_x AND shot_x < ship_x + 60 THEN
            IF shot_y > ship_y AND shot_y < ship_y + 60 THEN
                shooting = 0
                booming = 1
                boom_x = ship_x
                boom_y = ship_y
                ship_x = 800
            END IF
        END IF
        'hit sub1?
        IF shot_x > sub1_x AND shot_x < sub1_x + 60 THEN
            IF shot_y > sub1_y AND shot_y < sub1_y + 60 THEN
                shooting = 0
                booming = 1
                boom_x = sub1_x
                boom_y = sub1_y
                sub1_x = 800
            END IF
        END IF
        'hit sub2?
        IF shot_x > sub2_x AND shot_x < sub2_x + 60 THEN
            IF shot_x > sub2_y AND shot_y < sub2_y + 60 THEN
                shooting = 0
                booming = 1
                boom_x = sub2_x
                boom_y = sub2_y
                sub2_x = 800
            END IF
        END IF
    END IF
END IF
```

```
'explosion time?
IF booming = 1 THEN
    _PUTIMAGE (boom_x, boom_y), boom&
    _DISPLAY
    SLEEP 1 'pause for 1 second
    booming = 0
    score = score + 1
END IF

k$ = INKEY$
IF k$ = CHR$(27) THEN END
IF k$ = CHR$(32) AND shooting = 0 THEN
    shooting = 1
    shot_x = 400
    shot_y = 550
END IF
END SUB
```

Summary

Oops, this chapter didn't have much in common with squirt guns, lasers, or bazookas, unless you consider shooting underwater at ships sort of the same thing. Oh well, close enough! The good news is, you learned how to control several things at once in the game, and give each of the enemy ships their own speed.

There's a ton more things you could do to make this game better, though!

How about making two guns so two players can play at once! Or how about letting the ships drop depth charges at the player's gun or something? You might be ready to do some changes like this after a little more practice.

Quiz

Here is a little quiz to test whether you were paying attention. Try to answer the questions without looking up the answers first. This is not graded; it will just tell you whether you are ready to move on. The answers are found in Appendix A.

1. What statement do you use to call a sub-procedure or function?

A. RUN

B. CALL

C. DO

D. LOAD

2. How do you declare a global variable that can be used in any sub-procedure or function so that it is visible everywhere in the program?

A. DIM SHARED

B. PUBLIC

C. GLOBAL

D. VAR

3. How do you cause the program to pause for 1 second?

A. PAUSE 1

B. REST 1

C. SLEEP 1

D. BREAK 1

4. What command causes the screen to be refreshed immediately?

A. _REFRESH

B. _REDRAW

C. _UPDATE

D. _DISPLAY

5. What command fills a region of any shape with a solid color?

A. PAINT

B. FILL

C. DRAW

D. BUCKET

Homework

Your homework for this chapter is required to prove that you understand what you learned! If you have a hard time with this homework, then maybe you went too fast and might need to review the chapter again.

Instructions:

To increase the challenge of the game in this chapter, one way is to speed up the ship and subs as they move across the screen. See if you can find where in the code the ships are moved, and make it so they move *twice* as fast. That should make it much more difficult!

Chapter 9

Serious Samantha versus the Zillion Zombies

I n this chapter, you will learn an important new trick in video game programming: how to handle a ton of things in the game at once. For instance, showing a zillion zombies on the screen at once! This requires some programming wizardry that you'll learn in this chapter— a very useful skill indeed! Most video games display a lot of things on the screen at once. In a typical arcade game, these game objects are often called *sprites*. A *sprite* is a small game character that moves around and does something. For instance, a spaceship is a sprite; the plasma bolts that it fires are sprites; the alien ships that it fights against are sprites. We *are* going to do some basic animation in this chapter too—just enough to make the zombies look like they're walking.

Making a Sprite

Sometimes, when you're making a video game, there are just so many things to keep track of with variables that it becomes impossible! When this happens, it's time to start looking at a better way to keep track of the characters, monsters, spaceships, or what have you. Fortunately, BASIC lets us define our own custom user-defined type. Think of a TYPE as a group or container for a family of variables that are all closely related. Here is a TYPE called Sprite that we'll use for the game in this chapter:

```
TYPE Sprite
    alive AS INTEGER
    x AS INTEGER
    y AS INTEGER
    width AS INTEGER
    height AS INTEGER
END TYPE
```

The important thing to remember when making up your own TYPE is that the variables have to be specifically defined using AS—we can't get away with using a symbol like & (for a long integer) or $ (for a string).

You can put any variables you want inside your own custom TYPE definition! You can even make a special TYPE for different game objects. They don't all have to share the same one.

In the `sprite` group definition there are only integers (whole numbers, no decimal), but you can put any type of variable inside a `TYPE`. The `sprite` definition has these variables:

* `alive`—whether the sprite is alive (1) or not (0)
* `x`—the x coordinate of the sprite
* `y`—the y coordinate of the sprite
* `width`—the width of the sprite
* `height`—the height of the sprite

These properties would all have to be defined with globals were it not for the `TYPE` definition, `sprite`. Just think, for every object in the game, like a hero, dragon, tree, rock, or treasure chest, you would have to keep track of *every variable* for *every object*. So, you'd need a `hero_alive`, `hero_x`, `hero_y`, and so on, for every single one!

You would need a million variables for one big game! Okay, maybe a hundred or so, but a million is what it feels like when you're trying to manage them all!

Making *Lots* of Sprites

Now that you have a special `TYPE` for managing game objects, you can learn how to keep track of *lots* of game objects. For example, if you are making a space shoot-em-up game, where you have a spaceship and a lot of bad guys to shoot (usually evil aliens, not to mention random asteroids and power-ups!), that's a lot of stuff to keep track of. Even with the help of `sprite`, it's still too much to handle.

This is where you will learn a really awesome, totally advanced new trick passed down through the ages by the game programming gurus.

The trick is to use a *container* and `FOR` loops to manage tons of things in a game very easily.

The container I'm referring to is called an *array*. You create an array like this:

```
DIM asteroids(100)
```

That line creates an array called `asteroids` with room for 100 items or elements (numbered 1 to 100). Think of each item in the array as a little box, and all 100 boxes make up the "group" called `asteroids`.

 SECRET Arrays in BASIC start with 1. Some more advanced languages, like C++, use 0 as the start of an array. In BASIC we don't worry about such things.

Some of the boxes will be empty; some will be filled with data. It's *your job* as the programmer to use the boxes properly. We can't have any mismanaged array boxes here!

Now, let's say we want to draw all the objects in the *asteroids* array. Here is how you would do that:

```
FOR n = 1 to 100
    IF asteroids(n).alive = 1 THEN
        _PUTIMAGE (asteroids(n).x, asteroids(n).y), ↵
asteroid_image&
    END IF
NEXT n
```

See how the FOR loop goes through all 100 elements in the *asteroids* array? The IF line does a very important thing—it skips empty boxes in the array, and only draws those that are being used. So, when we start the game, it's a good idea to set the `alive` property (for all of the asteroids) to 0, until they are filled with real-life asteroids (and not just empty boxes).

 SECRET Here's an advanced feature you might use some time: You can resize an array using the REDIM statement. It is kind of slow to do this, so I don't recommend doing it inside the game loop.

Serious Samantha

Now I will show you how to make the game for this chapter! There are going to be a lot of sprites in this game! You will learn a good skill by working on this game—how to deal with a ton of sprites in a game! The explanation only goes so far; better to learn by doing it yourself. We'll be making this game in a single go, unlike the game in the previous chapter that was built in stages. A little variety makes things more interesting!

So, let's get started on this game. First up is the introductory code for the timer, the screen, and our `sprite` definition. Also in this section are the global variables. We have two groups of people in this game: the zombies and the survivors! Then there's the hero, controlled by the player, and another array called bullets. Does that give away too much? Well, if you can read the code at this early stage, then you can probably guess what this game is all about! But to take the guesswork out, let's see what the game looks like right away. See Figure 9.1.

Figure 9.1

The Serious Samantha game boasts a lot of sprites!

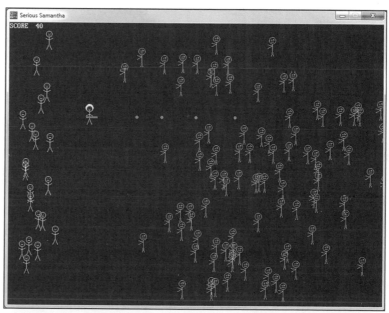

The Serious Samantha game is controlled using the Up/Down keys to move and the Space key to fire.

Let's get started. Type this code into a new program listing using QB64.

```
_TITLE "Serious Samantha"
RANDOMIZE TIMER
scrn& = _NEWIMAGE(800, 600, 32)
SCREEN scrn&

TYPE Sprite
    alive AS INTEGER
    x AS INTEGER
    y AS INTEGER
    width AS INTEGER
    height AS INTEGER
END TYPE

DIM sam AS Sprite
DIM zombie_frame&
DIM zombie&(2)
DIM zombie_mob(100) AS Sprite
DIM survivor_group(20) AS Sprite
DIM bullets(20) AS Sprite
```

Now that wraps up the introductory stuff required by the game. Next, we have all of the code to create the graphics. You should be used to this sort of code by now. First, we declare some colors using the _RGB() function, then create shapes and store them as images (thanks to the very useful _NEWIMAGE() function that creates an image). Then we draw on the new image.

Let's begin with the player sprite. The player is a woman carrying a huge gun (like her big brother, Serious Sam). She wears her hair up, not down, and it unfortunately looks a little bit like a helmet. I'm counting on your imagination here!

```
green& = _RGB(30, 255, 30)
black& = _RGB(0, 0, 0)
gunmetal& = _RGB(120, 120, 144)
orange& = _RGB(255, 140, 0)
red& = _RGB(255, 20, 20)
'make the player
samantha& = _NEWIMAGE(60, 60, 32)
_DEST samantha&
CIRCLE (20, 15), 8, green&
PAINT (20, 15), green&
CIRCLE (20, 17), 6, black&
PAINT (20, 17), black&
```

```
CIRCLE (20, 17), 6, green&
PSET (18, 15), green&
PSET (22, 15), green&
LINE (18, 19)-(22, 19), green&
LINE (18, 19)-(20, 21), green&
LINE (20, 21)-(22, 19), green&
LINE (20, 24)-(20, 38), green&
LINE (20, 28)-(13, 32), green&
LINE (20, 28)-(27, 32), green&
LINE (20, 38)-(15, 50), green&
LINE (20, 38)-(25, 50), green&
LINE (13, 33)-(37, 36), gunmetal&, BF
sam.x = 150
sam.y = 350
sam.width = 60
sam.height = 60
```

Next, we have the code to make a survivor. Yes, this game features a hero, zombies, and survivors. Can you guess what the game is about yet? Note that there are 20 survivors, and the array is called survivor_group.

```
'make a survivor
survivor& = _NEWIMAGE(60, 60, 32)
_DEST survivor&
CIRCLE (20, 17), 6, green&
PSET (18, 15), green&
PSET (22, 15), green&
LINE (18, 19)-(22, 19), green&
LINE (20, 24)-(20, 38), green&
LINE (20, 30)-(13, 26), green&
LINE (20, 30)-(27, 26), green&
LINE (20, 38)-(15, 50), green&
LINE (20, 38)-(25, 50), green&

FOR n = 1 TO 20
    survivor_group(n).alive = 1
    survivor_group(n).x = RND * 80
    survivor_group(n).y = RND * 540
    survivor_group(n).width = 60
    survivor_group(n).height = 60
NEXT n
```

Next, we create the zombie artwork! The zombies look truly diabolical, just ready to eat some brains! Be careful in this game—don't let them reach the survivors!

Now, there's one really great thing about this game that you have not seen in any previous chapter examples yet: animation! That's right, the zombies *animate* as they walk across the screen toward the brains—I mean, *survivors*. The image is made up of two frames—one frame standing normally, and another frame with the zombie taking one step forward. The animation array is called zombie, and has two elements or boxes in the array.

After the two frames of graphics for the zombie have been created, then we make the array for the group of zombies. You might call it a zombie horde of the apocalypse! There are 100 elements in the array, which is called zombie_mob.

```
'make a zombie
zombie&(1) = _NEWIMAGE(60, 60, 32)
_DEST zombie&(1)
CIRCLE (20, 17), 7, orange&
CIRCLE (18, 16), 1, orange&
CIRCLE (22, 16), 1, orange&
LINE (21, 14)-(24, 15), orange&
LINE (17, 20)-(23, 20), orange&
LINE (20, 24)-(20, 38), orange&
LINE (20, 28)-(10, 26), orange&
LINE (20, 28)-(10, 34), orange&
LINE (20, 38)-(15, 50), orange&
LINE (20, 38)-(25, 50), orange&

zombie&(2) = _NEWIMAGE(60, 60, 32)
_DEST zombie&(2)
CIRCLE (20, 17), 7, orange&
CIRCLE (18, 16), 1, orange&
CIRCLE (22, 16), 1, orange&
LINE (21, 14)-(24, 15), orange&
LINE (17, 20)-(23, 20), orange&
LINE (20, 24)-(20, 38), orange&
LINE (20, 28)-(10, 26), orange&
LINE (20, 28)-(10, 34), orange&
LINE (20, 38)-(18, 50), orange&
LINE (20, 38)-(22, 50), orange&
zombie_frame = 1

FOR n = 1 TO 100
    zombie_mob(n).alive = 1
    zombie_mob(n).x = 400 + RND * 400
    zombie_mob(n).y = RND * 540
    zombie_mob(n).width = 60
    zombie_mob(n).height = 60
NEXT n
```

Next, we create an array to keep track of bullets. This game is all about heavy firepower! You don't have to just fire one bullet and wait to fire again. No! In this game, you get a *machine gun!* You can hose the zombies! That's the fun part about it.

```
'make a bullet
bullet& = _NEWIMAGE(8, 8, 32)
_DEST bullet&
CIRCLE (4, 4), 3, red&
PAINT (4, 4), red&

FOR n = 1 TO 20
    bullets(n).alive = 0
    bullets(n).x = 0
    bullets(n).y = 0
    bullets(n).width = 8
    bullets(n).height = 8
NEXT n
```

Okay, we're done making all the graphics for the game, so now we can write the code to make the game work. First up is the start of the DO loop. Since this is the loop that continues running as long as the game is playing, we can call it our *game loop*. The first thing we do in the loop is draw the player, which is just one image.

```
score = 0
gameover = 0
_DEST scrn&
DO
    CLS

    'draw the player
    _PUTIMAGE (sam.x, sam.y), samantha&
```

Next in the game loop, we have to draw the survivors. This calls for a FOR loop that draws all 20 survivors in the survivor_group array. We don't care whether survivors are alive or not, because of the way the game plays. If the zombies get past Samantha, then the game is over—period. There's no room for error; if one survivor gets killed, then they are all pretty much toast. So, it's your job to prevent that from ever happening! If you aren't up to the challenge, then I recommend not running the game. It's just too sad when the worst happens.

```
'draw survivors
FOR n = 1 TO 20
    x = survivor_group(n).x
    y = survivor_group(n).y
    _PUTIMAGE (x, y), survivor&
NEXT n
```

Next, we have a FOR loop to draw all 100 zombies. In this case, again, we don't keep track of whether they are alive or not, we just draw them all. If you shoot a zombie with your gun, then it doesn't actually remove the zombie, it just makes them start over at the other side of the screen. This way, we *recycle* the zombies and it makes the game feel like there's a horde much bigger than just what you see on the screen.

```
'draw zombies
FOR n = 1 TO 100
    x = zombie_mob(n).x
    y = ombie_mob(n).y
    _PUTIMAGE (x, y), zombie&(zombie_frame)
NEXT n
```

Now, the next section of code is similar to the previous, but now we're *animating* the zombies, and moving them. This requires the use of a TIMER, because the zombies have to move at a certain rate. I've set it to 1/2 second per step. That means the zombies take two steps per second. It's slow enough that a good player should be able to stop them, but there are so *many* of them, it can be difficult if too many are walking toward you at once. If you fail, you might be left for dead, I'm sorry to say.

```
'animate and move zombies
IF TIMER - anim_timer >= 0.5 THEN
    zombie_frame = zombie_frame + 1
    IF zombie_frame > 2 THEN zombie_frame = 1
    anim_timer = TIMER
    FOR n = 1 TO 100
        zombie_mob(n).x = zombie_mob(n).x - 4
        IF zombie_mob(n).x < 100 THEN gameover = 1
    NEXT n
END IF
```

Next up in the game loop is the code to draw the bullets. Now *this* is some fun code! Bullets have to be recycled. What this means is, whenever you shoot a bullet, it moves until one of two things occur: 1) The bullet hits a zombie; 2) The bullet goes off the screen. When either event happens, the bullet is *recycled*. By recycled, I mean, the `alive` property is set to 0.

To fire the gun, press the Space key. It's a rapid-fire machine gun! This works by using the `bullets` array. Every time you press the Space key, the game looks through the array with a FOR loop until it finds an unused bullet. A bullet is not being used when `alive = 0`. But, we're getting ahead of ourselves... First, let's just draw all the bullets that have been shot.

```
'draw and move bullets
FOR n = 1 TO 20
    IF bullets(n).alive = 1 THEN
        _PUTIMAGE (bullets(n).x, bullets(n).y), bullet&
        bullets(n).x = bullets(n).x + 2
        IF bullets(n).x > 800 THEN bullets(n).alive = 0
    END IF
NEXT n
```

Next, display the score. You gain a point every time you take down a zombie! At this point, we also called on _DISPLAY to refresh the screen. That's the end of drawing.

```
'show the score
_PRINTMODE _KEEPBACKGROUND
_PRINTSTRING (0, 0), "SCORE " + STR$(score)

_DISPLAY
```

Next up in our game loop is the code to check for when a bullet hits a zombie. When this happens, the bullet is removed (by setting `alive = 0`), and the zombie is moved to the back of the line (off the right side of the screen).

```
'see if bullets hit any zombies
FOR b = 1 TO 20
    IF bullets(b).alive = 1 THEN
        FOR z = 1 TO 100
            c = Collision(bullets(b), zombie_mob(z))
            IF c = 1 THEN
                score = score + 1
                bullets(b).alive = 0
                zombie_mob(z).x = zombie_mob(z).x + 400
            END IF
        NEXT z
    END IF
NEXT b
```

Now we are ready for the keyboard input. This is the section of code that handles user input. For this game, use the Up and Down arrow keys to move Samantha up or down. Use the Space key to fire her gun! That's it! Oh, and also, you can quit by pressing the Escape key.

```
k$ = INKEY$
IF k$ <> "" THEN
    code = ASC(k$)
    IF code = 0 THEN
        'detect arrow keys
        code = ASC(k$, 2)
        IF code = 72 THEN 'up
            sam.y = sam.y - 8
            IF sam.y < 0 THEN sam.y = 0
        ELSEIF code = 80 THEN 'down
            sam.y = sam.y + 8
            IF sam.y > 540 THEN sam.y = 540
        END IF
    ELSEIF code = 32 THEN 'space
        FOR n = 1 TO 20
            IF bullets(n).alive = 0 THEN
                bullets(n).alive = 1
                bullets(n).x = sam.x + sam.width / 2
                bullets(n).y = sam.y + sam.height / 2
                EXIT FOR
            END IF
        NEXT n
    ELSEIF code = 27 THEN 'escape
        gameover = 1
    END IF
END IF
LOOP UNTIL gameover = 1
_PRINTSTRING (350, 0), "OH NO, THE ZOMBIES GOT THROUGH!"
_PRINTSTRING (350, 20), "GAME OVER, MAN! GAME OVER!"
_DISPLAY
END
```

That last bit of code after the LOOP statement requires a little explanation. Since we're outside the game loop now, there will be no more calls to _DISPLAY. So, we have to print out the results of the game (i.e., "you lose"). Then, to make that message appear, you have to call _DISPLAY one more time.

Finally, we're almost done! The last portion of the program is the Collision function. This function checks two Sprite objects to see if they are hitting each other. You know that one Sprite is hitting another Sprite when they are overlapping each other. That is, when one is partially over the top of the other one.

The way this function works is, we get the center of the first sprite: cx and cy. Using this center point, we then check the second sprite to see if the center point is anywhere inside its borders.

How do you check the borders of a Sprite? By looking at its x and y coordinates, and its width and height properties.

```
FUNCTION Collision (sprite1 AS Sprite, sprite2 AS Sprite)
Collision = 0
cx = sprite1.x + sprite1.width / 2
cy = sprite1.y + sprite1.height / 2
IF cx > sprite2.x AND cx < sprite2.x + sprite2.width THEN
    IF cy > sprite2.y AND cy < sprite2.y + sprite2.height THEN
        Collision = 1
        EXIT FUNCTION
    END IF
END IF
END FUNCTION
```

Anyway, when you're all done typing in the program, go ahead and give it a run! See if you can beat my high score! It's shown in Figure 9.2. See there, I took out 53 zombies before they got past my defensive line and attacked the survivors. Doh!

Figure 9.2

Oh no, the zombie horde has attacked the survivors!

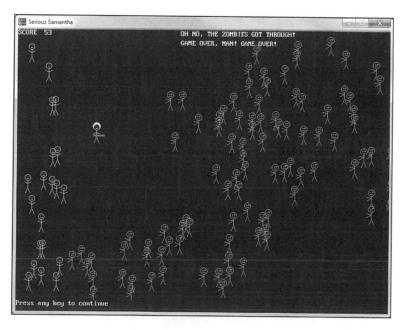

Summary

That wraps up the chapter on *tons of objects* and *fancy collision detection*. I hope you like these subjects because in the next three chapters, you'll be doing a lot more of it! I have something very special planned for those upcoming games!

Quiz

Here is a little quiz to test whether you were paying attention. Try to answer the questions without looking up the answers first. This is not graded; it will just tell you whether you are ready to go to the next chapter. The answers are found in Appendix A.

1. What BASIC looping statement do we use in this chapter to draw a whole array of Sprites?

A. FOR...NEXT

B. DO...LOOP

C. DO...UNTIL

D. DO...WHILE

2. What special technique does the game use to make the zombies seem to walk?

A. Filtering

B. Rotation

C. Animation

D. Zooming

3. What is the proper programming term for when two sprites hit each other?

A. Crash

B. Collision

C. Bump

D. Smash

4. What command causes graphics output to go to a certain image?

A. _DEST

B. _TARGET

C. _IMAGE

D. _OUTPUT

5. How would you declare an array of 50 Sprites called ants?

A. DIM Sprite (AS ants)

B. DIM ants AS Sprite(50)

C. DIM Sprite AS ants(50)

D. DIM ants(50) AS Sprite

Homework

Your homework for this chapter is required to prove that you understand what you learned! If you have a hard time with this homework, then maybe you went too fast, and you might need to review the chapter again.

Instructions:

You are going to conduct an experiment to see how fast BASIC works. Start a new program file. Using one of the bitmap files in the game (such as the beetle.png file), create an array of 1,000 sprites, and draw them exactly as they are in the game. When a beetle reaches the left edge, cause it to wrap around to the right again, as it does in the game. Be mindful of which code you need in your program to move and draw all 1,000 sprites.

Chapter 10

Ron's Ridiculous
Bludger Battle

W e're going to take a break from making games about *people* and cover some other subjects for a while. I want to return to the idea behind the game we made back in Chapter 5 called Cannonball Carl. There's so much potential in that simple game, and I want to show you a different way of playing a similar game—where you have a ball and blocks. Instead of a cannon, the player will control a *paddle*. This type of game is often called a "ball & paddle" game. This will give you more good experience with a game loop, collision detection, and fast gameplay, among other things.

Better Sprites

Remember the old Sprite TYPE we made? It does a pretty good job of keeping track of a sprite, but it doesn't do very much other than that. You're going to improve Sprite by giving it some new features! The most common thing that a sprite does is draw somewhere on the screen. Now, it will have a built-in image property!

Also, to make it easier to move sprites around, Sprite now has a pair of properties for movement: speed_x and speed_y!

```
TYPE Sprite
    alive AS INTEGER
    x AS INTEGER
    y AS INTEGER
    width AS INTEGER
    height AS INTEGER
    speed_x AS SINGLE
    speed_y AS SINGLE
    image AS LONG
END TYPE
```

Instead of using a separate variable for making the image for a sprite (like we did in the Serious Samantha game), now the image is built in! Here is a good example:

```
DIM dog AS Sprite
dog.image = _NEWIMAGE(60, 60, 32)
```

In this example, we can just use dog.image directly from inside the Sprite itself. This is a big improvement!

There is a bunch of new code for doing special things with sprites that you'll learn about in the game, so let's get started on those helpers right away.

Drawing Sprites

You can use this new helpful sub-procedure to draw a sprite by simply sending it the `sprite` variable (assuming `image` has been set properly ahead of time).

```
SUB SpriteDraw (spr AS Sprite)
_PUTIMAGE (spr.x, spr.y), spr.image
END SUB
```

 The example game coming up will show these subs in the correct location in the program, so you don't have to type this in just yet. Just focus on studying the code for these new "helper" subs!

Moving Sprites

You can use this helper sub-procedure to *move* a sprite. This works thanks to the new `speed_x` and `speed_y` properties!

```
SUB SpriteMove (spr AS Sprite)
spr.x = spr.x + spr.speed_x
spr.y = spr.y + spr.speed_y
END SUB
```

Crashing Sprites

You learned how to check for when two things crash into each other already. But there's a better way to do it. This new `SpriteCollision` function checks both sprites you send to it, not just the first one (like the old function did).

There are more advanced ways to tell when two game objects hit each other, but this is probably the easiest way of them all. We just look at the center of each sprite and determine whether it is touching the other sprite.

```
FUNCTION SpriteCollision (spr1 AS Sprite, spr2 AS Sprite)
SpriteCollision = 0
'test first sprite
cx = spr1.x + spr1.width / 2
cy = spr1.y + spr1.height / 2
IF cx > spr2.x AND cx < spr2.x + spr2.width THEN
```

```
            IF cy > spr2.y AND cy < spr2.y + spr2.height THEN
                SpriteCollision = 1
                EXIT FUNCTION
            END IF
        END IF
    END IF
    'test second sprite
    cx = spr2.x + spr2.width / 2
    cy = spr2.y + spr2.height / 2
    IF cx > spr1.x AND cx < spr1.x + spr1.width THEN
        IF cy > spr1.y AND cy < spr1.y + spr1.height THEN
            SpriteCollision = 1
            EXIT FUNCTION
        END IF
    END IF
    END FUNCTION
```

One of the advanced types of collision detection mentioned before is called *spherical-* or *radial-* or *distance*-based collision. The three different names mean the same thing—the distance between two objects is the same as drawing a circle around each one and seeing if the circles touch. If they do, it's a collision.

Bouncing Sprites

Commonly, sprites need to bounce off of things—like the walls or other sprites. Here is a helper sub-procedure that can do that. You send it the sprite you want it to check, and then the boundary (minx, miny) to (maxx, maxy). Then, this code makes sure the sprite stays *inside* that boundary. In the game in this chapter, this sub-procedure is used to keep the ball inside the screen. But you could use it for other purposes too, like keeping an enemy from going outside of a certain range of the screen.

```
SUB SpriteBounce (spr AS Sprite, minx, miny, maxx, maxy)
IF spr.x < minx THEN
    spr.x = minx
    spr.speed_x = -spr.speed_x
ELSEIF spr.x > maxx THEN
    spr.x = maxx
    spr.speed_x = -spr.speed_x
END IF
IF spr.y < miny THEN
    spr.y = miny
```

```
        spr.speed_y = -spr.speed_y
ELSEIF spr.y > maxy THEN
        spr.y = maxy
        spr.speed_y = -spr.speed_y
END IF
END SUB
```

The Bludger Battle Game

There are a few new things we're going to do to make the source code for the game in this chapter easier to understand. First, this game uses SUBS and FUNCTIONS. You haven't seen very much of them in quite a while, but this game is large enough that they are a big help. Second, all of the code has great comments in it—especially the SUBS and FUNCTIONS. This should make it easier to see what each part of the program does. Third, there are a bunch of new sprite sub-procedures that you can use in your own games!

Let's start off by taking a look at the game. Figure 10.1 shows the game running.

Figure 10.1

The "Bludger Battle" game is a typical "Ball & Paddle"-type game.

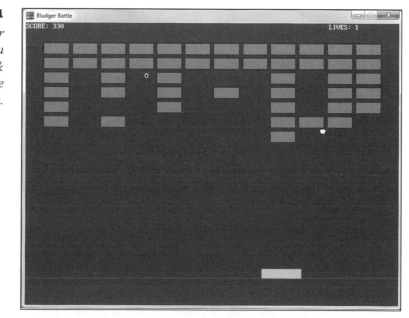

The goal of the game is to clear the level by knocking out all of the blocks using the ball and your paddle (controlled by the mouse). When the game first starts up, it's in waiting = 1 mode, where the ball goes with the paddle until you click the mouse button. Then it goes into `waiting = 0` mode where the ball goes off toward the blocks. This is shown in Figure 10.2.

Figure 10.2

When you miss the ball, the game goes into a wait mode.

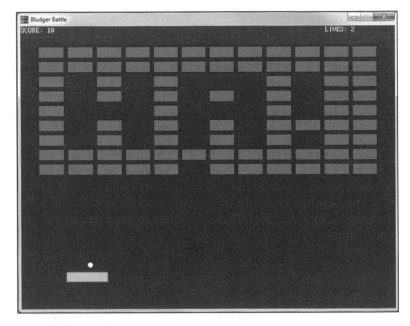

Any time the ball hits something—whether it's the paddle, blocks, or walls—it will bounce off and go the opposite direction. A special case is when the ball hits a block. To keep the game easy to understand, the ball will always bounce *down* away from a block, even if it hits a block from above or from the side.

A more complex paddle game could look at where the ball hits a block and have it bounce off any side—top, bottom, or sides—realistically. That takes a lot of code, though, and we just want to make the game without it getting too serious!

This is the complete source code for the Bludger Battle game. If you prefer to wimp out and load the file instead, it is called BludgerBattle.bas. If you're wondering where the name comes from, I'll give you a hint: it's from a book written by J. K. Rowling. (See the Introduction for instructions on downloading the files.)

Let's build the game, one piece at a time. First, the usual introductory things like variables and such.

```
'********************
' Bludger Battle Game
'********************

_TITLE "Bludger Battle"

TYPE Sprite
    alive AS INTEGER
    x AS INTEGER
    y AS INTEGER
    width AS INTEGER
    height AS INTEGER
    speed_x AS SINGLE
    speed_y AS SINGLE
    image AS LONG
END TYPE

DIM SHARED scrn&
DIM SHARED paddle AS Sprite
DIM SHARED ball AS Sprite
DIM SHARED block_count, block_image&
DIM SHARED level(13, 5) AS INTEGER
DIM SHARED blocks(120) AS Sprite
DIM SHARED background AS Sprite
DIM score, gameover, waiting, lives
```

Next, we call some helper sub-procedures to make the program look nicer. This way, you can tell exactly what each sub is doing just by name, and it keeps *this* part of the program looking more tidy.

```
CALL InitGame
CALL MakeBackground
CALL MakePaddle
CALL MakeBlock
CALL MakeBall
CALL BuildLevel
```

Now we come to the game loop. There are some variables set here for the game's logic—like the score, your lives, etc. The first thing that happens inside the loop is several things are drawn right away. That's the background, the paddle, and the ball. The background is a really neat addition in this game that you have not seen before. I'll go over it when we come to the MakeBackground sub.

```
'********************
' GAME LOOP
'********************
_DEST scrn&
score = 0
waiting = 1
lives = 3
gameover = 0
DO UNTIL gameover = 1
    CALL SpriteDraw(background) 'draw background
    CALL SpriteDraw(paddle) 'draw paddle
    CALL SpriteDraw(ball) 'draw ball
```

Next up is the code to draw the blocks, and a check to see when the level has been cleared (when you knock out all the blocks). Also in this section is the code that prints the score and lives on the screen.

```
'draw the blocks
total = 0
FOR n = 1 TO block_count
    IF blocks(n).alive = 1 THEN
        total = total + 1
        CALL SpriteDraw(blocks(n))
    END IF
NEXT n

'see if level is cleared
IF total = 0 THEN
    _PRINTSTRING (350, 350), "GAME OVER"
    _DISPLAY
    SLEEP
    gameover = 1
END IF

_PRINTMODE _KEEPBACKGROUND
_PRINTSTRING (0, 0), "SCORE:" + STR$(score)
_PRINTSTRING (650, 0), "LIVES:" + STR$(lives)
'finish doing graphics
_DISPLAY
```

That wraps up all of the drawing needs for this game. Now we can focus on the game logic. Logic is to a program what an engine is to a car—it makes things *go*! In the logic for our Bludger Battle game (which is hardly a battle, but it just sounded like a good name), we have to cause the ball to move and bounce off things, and destroy the blocks. That's what all of this next bit of code does.

```
'move the ball
IF waiting = 0 THEN 'wait for player to start
    CALL SpriteMove(ball)
    CALL SpriteBounce(ball, 0, 0, 780, 580)
ELSE
    ball.x = paddle.x + paddle.width / 2
    ball.y = paddle.y - 20
END IF

'check for ball-paddle collision
IF SpriteCollision(ball, paddle) = 1 THEN
    ball.y = paddle.y - ball.height
    ball.speed_y = -ball.speed_y
END IF

'check for ball-block collisions
FOR n = 1 TO block_count
    IF blocks(n).alive = 1 THEN
        IF SpriteCollision(blocks(n), ball) = 1 THEN
            score = score + 10
            blocks(n).alive = 0
            ball.speed_y = ABS(ball.speed_y)
        END IF
    END IF
NEXT n
```

Good! You're making huge progress very quickly. The great thing about this game is, you can do a lot without writing a ton of code thanks to the subs and functions—but we'll come to them in a minute. For the moment, let's focus on checking when the player misses the ball. If the ball goes down below the paddle, then you lose a "life." When that happens, the game goes into waiting = 1 mode. This mode causes the ball to just follow the paddle until you click the mouse button.

```
'check whether player lost the ball
IF ball.y > paddle.y + paddle.height THEN
    waiting = 1
    lives = lives - 1
    IF lives = 0 THEN gameover = 1
END IF
```

That wraps up all of the logic. The last bit of code inside the game loop is just "housekeeping" sort of code—getting mouse input and keyboard input.

```
'check mouse movement
mouse = _MOUSEINPUT
paddle.x = _MOUSEX
IF paddle.x < 10 THEN paddle.x = 10
IF paddle.x > 700 THEN paddle.x = 700

'check mouse buttons
IF _MOUSEBUTTON(1) <> 0 THEN
    waiting = 0
END IF

'check keys
k$ = INKEY$
IF k$ <> "" THEN
    IF k$ = CHR$(27) THEN gameover = 1
END IF
LOOP
END
```

Okay! Now you're done with the game loop, and we can go over all of the helper subs and functions. Let's start with InitGame.

```
'*******************
' InitGame Sub
'*******************
SUB InitGame
scrn& = _NEWIMAGE(800, 600, 32)
SCREEN scrn&
RANDOMIZE TIMER
_MOUSEHIDE
END SUB
```

Next, we have perhaps the most complex part of the program: BuildLevel. This sub uses the DATA statements to construct the level. A "level" in this game is the layout of the blocks. You can change the blocks to your own design if you want! Just take a look at the 1s and 0s in the DATA lines. The 1s are solid blocks; the 0s are empty spaces. Why don't you make your own picture using the blocks? Go ahead and design your own custom level!

The way BuildLevel works is by using an array called blocks, which is defined as Sprite. It looks at the DATA and sets each block sprite in the position where it belongs on the screen, by using the x and y properties. Take a look at the two FOR loops. The first one goes through the data rows (that is, the up to down direction). The next FOR loop goes through the columns (that is, the left to right direction). For every 0 or 1, a sprite is created in the location on the screen that looks somewhat like the level.

```
'********************
' BuildLevel Sub
'********************
DATA 1,1,1,1,1,1,1,1,1,1,1,1
DATA 1,1,1,1,1,1,1,1,1,1,1,1
DATA 1,0,1,0,1,0,0,0,1,0,1,1
DATA 1,0,1,0,1,0,1,0,1,0,1,1
DATA 1,0,0,0,1,0,0,0,1,0,1,1
DATA 1,0,1,0,1,0,1,0,1,1,1,1
DATA 1,0,1,0,1,0,1,0,1,0,1,1
DATA 1,1,1,1,1,1,1,1,1,1,1,1
DATA 1,1,1,1,1,1,1,1,1,1,1,1

SUB BuildLevel ()
block_count = 1
FOR row = 0 TO 8
    FOR col = 0 TO 11
        READ block_data
        i = block_count
        blocks(i).alive = block_data
        blocks(i).x = 34 + col * 61
        blocks(i).y = 40 + row * 31
        blocks(i).width = 60
        blocks(i).height = 30
        blocks(i).image = block_image&
        block_count = block_count + 1
    NEXT col
NEXT row
END SUB
```

Now we come to the "make" subs, which have the job of creating the graphics used in the game. The MakeBackground sub is really interesting! It is the first time you've used a solid background image in a game. In all the previous examples, we just used CLS to clear the screen. The background looks really great! It was created with a FOR loop. Inside this loop a series of boxes are created with the LINE statement (using the BF modifier—which means "box/filled"). Those boxes are drawn onto a full-size image the size of the window (800 × 600).

The rest of the "make" subs just make the paddle, ball, and blocks—nothing surprising here that you haven't seen before.

```
'********************
' MakeBackground Sub
'********************
```

Video Game Programming for Kids

```
SUB MakeBackground
background.x = 0
background.y = 0
background.width = 800
background.height = 600
background.image = _NEWIMAGE(800, 600, 32)
_DEST background.image
FOR y = 0 TO 599 STEP 4
    c& = _RGB(y / 10, y / 10, 256 - y / 10 * 3)
    LINE (0, y)-(799, y + 4), c&, BF
NEXT y
END SUB

'*******************
' MakePaddle Sub
'*******************
SUB MakePaddle
paddle.image = _NEWIMAGE(90, 24, 32)
_DEST paddle.image
LINE (0, 0)-(89, 23), _RGB(20, 90, 90), BF
LINE (2, 2)-(87, 21), _RGB(20, 220, 220), BF
paddle.x = 350
paddle.y = 520
paddle.width = 90
paddle.height = 24
END SUB
'*******************
' MakeBlock Sub
'*******************
SUB MakeBlock
block_image& = _NEWIMAGE(60, 30, 32)
_DEST block_image&
LINE (0, 0)-(59, 29), _RGB(90, 20, 90), BF
LINE (4, 4)-(55, 25), _RGB(220, 20, 220), BF
END SUB

'*******************
' MakeBall Sub
'*******************
SUB MakeBall
white& = _RGB(255, 255, 255)
ball.image = _NEWIMAGE(12, 12, 32)
_DEST ball.image
CIRCLE (6, 6), 5, white&
PAINT (6, 6), white&
ball.x = 350
ball.y = 500
ball.width = 24
ball.height = 24
```

174

```
ball.speed_x = 0.7
ball.speed_y = 1.4
END SUB
```

Alright, now you're getting into the new sprite subs and functions! Since we already went over these earlier, I'll just show them to you in the order that they appear in the game code (for the sake of completeness).

```
'*******************
' DrawSprite Sub
'*******************
SUB SpriteDraw (spr AS Sprite)
_PUTIMAGE (spr.x, spr.y), spr.image
END SUB


'*******************
' MoveSprite Sub
'*******************
SUB SpriteMove (spr AS Sprite)
spr.x = spr.x + spr.speed_x
spr.y = spr.y + spr.speed_y
END SUB


'************************
' SpriteCollision Function
'************************
FUNCTION SpriteCollision (spr1 AS Sprite, spr2 AS
Sprite)
SpriteCollision = 0
'test first sprite
cx = spr1.x + spr1.width / 2
cy = spr1.y + spr1.height / 2
IF cx > spr2.x AND cx < spr2.x + spr2.width THEN
    IF cy > spr2.y AND cy < spr2.y + spr2.height THEN
        SpriteCollision = 1
        EXIT FUNCTION
    END IF
END IF
'test second sprite
cx = spr2.x + spr2.width / 2
cy = spr2.y + spr2.height / 2
IF cx > spr1.x AND cx < spr1.x + spr1.width THEN
    IF cy > spr1.y AND cy < spr1.y + spr1.height THEN
        SpriteCollision = 1
        EXIT FUNCTION
    END IF
END IF
```

```
END FUNCTION

'********************
' SpriteBounce Sub
'********************
SUB SpriteBounce (spr AS Sprite, minx, miny, maxx, maxy)
IF spr.x < minx THEN
    spr.x = minx
    spr.speed_x = -spr.speed_x
ELSEIF spr.x > maxx THEN
    spr.x = maxx
    spr.speed_x = -spr.speed_x
END IF
IF spr.y < miny THEN
    spr.y = miny
    spr.speed_y = -spr.speed_y
ELSEIF spr.y > maxy THEN
    spr.y = maxy
    spr.speed_y = -spr.speed_y
END IF
END SUB
```

To wrap up the game, we'll take a look at one last figure. This screen shown in Figure 10.3 shows the level cleared! When this happens, the game ends. It's a short but sweet game!

Figure 10.3

You win the game by clearing all the blocks.

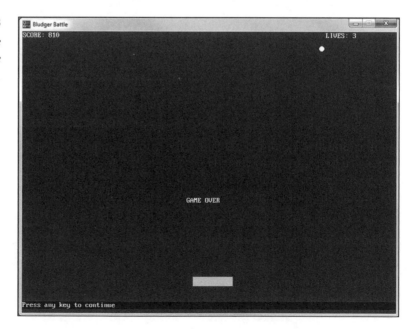

Summary

In this chapter you were able to see how a mature sprite system works, with a custom `sprite` structure and helper subs and functions to go with it. This is the start of a full-blown game sprite engine. But, we don't want to get ahead of ourselves and do too much too quickly. It's more important to develop programming skills than to create awe-inspiring games. Trust me! Work on simple games like the ones we've been creating in this book, and in no time you will be making your own from *scratch*!

Quiz

Here is a little quiz to test whether you were paying attention. Try to answer the questions without looking up the answers first. This is not graded; it will just tell you whether you are ready to go to the next chapter.. The answers are found in Appendix A.

1. Which of these is the correct code to define a Sprite variable?

A. Sprite dog

B. VAR dog (Sprite)

C. DIM dog (Sprite)

D. DIM dog AS Sprite

2. What command do you use to draw an image?

A. _DRAW

B. _PUTIMAGE

C. _PAINT

D. _DRAWIMG

3. Which of the following is the correct way to run a function called MakePaddle?

A. RUN MakePaddle

B. GOTO MakePaddle

C. CALL MakePaddle

D. JUMP MakePaddle

4. How do you check for a collision between two sprites?

A. By checking whether their borders overlap.

B. By checking the edge of the screen.

C. By checking the width and height of the sprites.

D. By checking the speed of the sprite.

5. What statement do you use to define the data for a game level?

A. LEVEL

B. LOAD

C. DATA

D. DEF

Homework

Your homework for this chapter is required to prove that you understand what you learned! If you have a hard time with this homework, then maybe you went too fast and might need to review the chapter again.

Instructions:

Modify the Bludger Battle game with your own level design. You will need to edit the DATA statements. Any space where you want a block to appear, use a "1"; a "0" means no block. Make your own creative level design and have your friends try it out.

Chapter 11

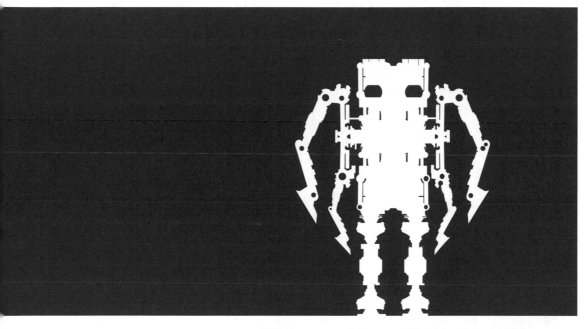

Attack of the Alien Beetles

T his chapter is completely different from all those that came before. Different is not always a good thing, but in this case different is most definitely better! You are going to learn to use bitmap artwork loaded from files rather than drawn with graphics statements like LINE. You've made some very good games with graphics, but now I want to show you how to make a game using graphics *loaded from a file*.

The only problem with loading graphics is that you need to have the file in order for the game to work. If you don't have the bitmap files for the game, it won't run. So, I'll show you first where to get the bitmaps (the artwork) for the game, and where to put it. If you have a hard time copying files on your PC, you might ask a parent or teacher to help you copy the files into the right place. The rule is generally this: put the bitmap files in the same directory as the .BAS file for your game.

Loading a Bitmap

You can load a bitmap file using the _LOADIMAGE statement. After loading, the image is treated like any other image. You have been using images for game graphics all along. But, instead of loading images, you have been creating them using _NEWIMAGE. The result is the same—the very same image is either created or loaded. To load a bitmap file as an image, it goes like this:

```
bitmap& = _LOADIMAGE("image.jpg")
_PUTIMAGE (0,0), bitmap&
```

The filename of the bitmap file is the only parameter you need to use. There are a lot of different file formats that BASIC supports (via QB64), including these:

* BMP
* JPG
* PNG
* TGA
* GIF
* PCX
* TIF

* LBM
* PNM
* XPM
* XCF

Some of these bitmap formats are familiar because they're used every day on the web and in digital cameras, but some are unusual. I think the overall best format to use for games is PNG—portable network graphics. PNG is very popular today for many reasons. First, it is high quality, but the file size is still pretty small. Like a JPG, a PNG is compressed to save memory. But like a BMP, a PNG does not lose any pixels due to compression.

Some formats, namely JPG, are a bad choice for a video game because a JPG image is messed up when it gets saved. What I mean is, the pixels of a JPG are changed to save memory, to increase the compression. This is why most JPGs are quite small, and they are preferred on the web. But, you sacrifice quality in return for small size.

JPG works *great* for photos, because you really can't tell that some pixels have been changed. But, with video game graphics, every pixel counts. If you were to save your spaceship image as a JPG, it's likely the laser cannon would be changed into a little blob of pixels. Small, highly detailed images (the likes of which are needed for a video game) are not suitable for JPG.

The Windows BMP format is pretty good. Like PNG, a BMP doesn't lose any detail when it is saved, and actually BMP images are *not compressed*. So, while quality is high, the file size is quite large. And, there's no support for an alpha channel transparency layer.

Transparency is very important in video game graphics. Otherwise, the background of the image gets drawn onto the screen. That only works if you don't care about the background—it's, like, black. But, usually you do care about the background in most games.

SECRET By default, QB64 is installed to C:\QB64. This is a directory on the *root* of the C: drive (on your computer's hard drive). This is where all programs go when compiled. When you press F5 to run a BASIC program, a compiler takes your BASIC code and converts it into an executable (.EXE) file. That is always created in C:\QB64. QB64 does not use "projects" or "output directories," because it was modeled after old, old BASIC.

The easiest way to load your bitmap files is to just copy them to the QB64 directory at C:\QB64. Another way is to tell _LOADIMAGE exactly where the bitmap file is located, like this:

```
img& = _LOADIMAGE("C:\MyGames\ship.png")
```

Drawing a Bitmap

Let's learn how to load and draw a bitmap from a file by writing a program to do it. There's a bit of a problem with the bitmap file location that I'll explain in a minute. First, let's find a bitmap file to use. You can use any image you want for this program, such as a personal photo from a digital camera, an image from a website—any image you want to use.

If you aren't sure how to save a bitmap file, sometimes you can do it by just right-clicking on an image, and choosing Save Image As. The *Secret* above explains where to store the bitmap files for your BASIC games.

Let's see the program that loads and draws an image. When you run the program, it will load the file ship_white.png, shown in Figure 11.1.

```
 1: _TITLE "Bitmap Demo"
 2:
 3: scrn& = _NEWIMAGE(800, 600, 32)
 4: SCREEN scrn&
 5:
 6: ship& = _LOADIMAGE("ship_white.png")
 7:
 8: w = _WIDTH(ship&)
 9: h = _HEIGHT(ship&)
10: x = 400 - w / 2
11: y = 300 - h / 2
```

```
12: _PUTIMAGE (x, y), ship&
13:
14: _DISPLAY
15: SLEEP
16: END
```

Figure 11.1

This spaceship bitmap has a white background and is not transparent.

Did the spaceship show up as shown, with a white border around it? If BASIC can't find the bitmap file (ship_white.png), then it will come up with this error message: "Invalid handle" (see Figure 11.2).

This error happens on the _WIDTH line, because the image is invalid (we can't get its width if it doesn't exist). When BASIC can't find the bitmap file, it doesn't just quit; it keeps running, but the image handle (ship&) is invalid, because the image wasn't loaded properly.

Now let's replace the ship_white.png with a bitmap that has a transparent background. This file is called just ship.png, and it has a transparent background. Take a look at this picture showing ship.png loaded into a picture editor. See Figure 11.3. Notice how the background around the ship has a checkerboard pattern? That means it's transparent.

Figure 11.2

*This error comes
up if BASIC can't
find the bitmap
file. It has to go in
the C:\QB64
folder.*

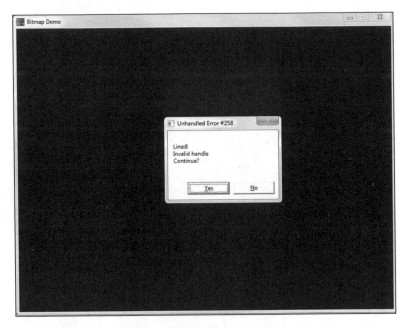

Once you have a bitmap file in the right folder, loading and drawing is pretty easy.

Let's try drawing the transparent ship instead. To do that, you'll
have to edit the program. Change the ship_white.png filename
with just ship.png as shown here:

```
ship& = _LOADIMAGE("ship.png")
```

Be sure to copy the ship.png file into C:\QB64, and then run the
program again. If the file is in the right folder, the program should
come up like this (see Figure 11.4).

Since the window's background is also black, you can't really tell
that the ship.png file has a transparent alpha channel. Let's make
a small change to the program so that the background isn't black.

Go back to the Bitmap Demo program (BitmapDemo.bas) and
add one line to clear the screen.

Figure 11.3

A transparent image hides the background.

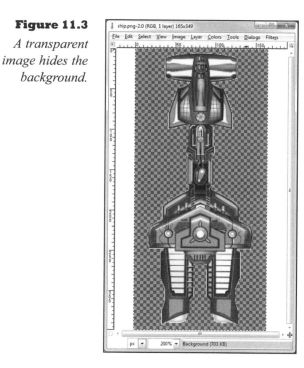

Figure 11.4

The spaceship with a transparent background (black).

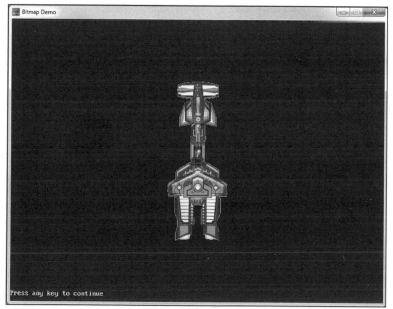

SECRET Remember how you have used _RGB to create a color with three numbers? Like, _RGB(255, 255, 255) equals white. Well, there's a *fourth* color component, and it's called *alpha*. That is where we get the name *alpha channel*. Each channel in a color is 8 bits, so with 4 channels, there are 8 × 4 = 32 bits. That's where you get "32-bit color."

You can use cls with a background color. Notice that there's a comma right after the cls—that's weird, but it tells BASIC to ignore the foreground and only change the background color. Add the cls line to the program below the screen line like this:

```
scrn& = _NEWIMAGE(800, 600, 32)
SCREEN scrn&
CLS , _RGB(0, 100, 100) 'be sure to add the 1st comma
```

Run the new and improved program, and it should look like Figure 11.5.

Figure 11.5

The ship is obviously transparent with a solid color on the background.

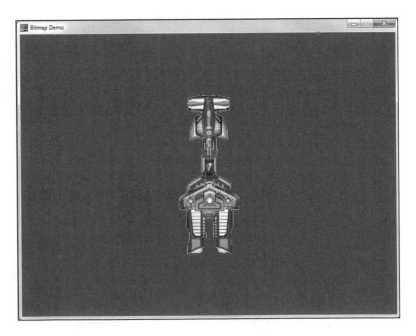

Drawing Stars

Now I want to show you a cool trick. This is a way you can draw stars on the background so that it looks like a spaceship is flying through space. This gives the sense of movement without actually moving the background—only little dots are being drawn. First, let's just write the program and then talk about it afterward.

```
_TITLE "Starfield"
scrn& = _NEWIMAGE(800, 600, 32)
SCREEN scrn&

TYPE Star
    x AS SINGLE
    y AS SINGLE
    brightness AS INTEGER
    speed AS SINGLE
END TYPE

DIM stars(100) AS Star
DIM b AS SINGLE

'create the stars
FOR n = 1 TO 100
    stars(n).x = RND * 800
    stars(n).y = RND * 600
    b = 50 + RND * 200
    stars(n).brightness = b
    stars(n).speed = b / 1000.0
NEXT n

DO
    CLS
    FOR n = 1 TO 100
        b = stars(n).brightness
        x = stars(n).x
        y = stars(n).y
        LINE (x - 1, y - 1)-(x + 1, y + 1), _RGB(b, b,
b), BF
        stars(n).x = stars(n).x - stars(n).speed
        IF stars(n).x < 0 THEN stars(n).x = 800
    NEXT n
    _DISPLAY
LOOP UNTIL INKEY$ <> ""
END
```

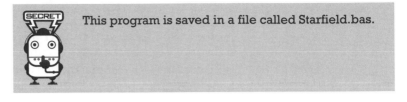

This program is saved in a file called Starfield.bas.

Now you can run the program by pressing F5. The program looks like Figure 11.6. If you look carefully you will see different colored dots in the picture. It's hard to tell on paper, but if you run the program it will make sense.

Figure 11.6

Drawing moving stars to simulate moving through space (like Star Trek).

Each star has its own brightness and speed properties. Brightness is a random number from 50 to 250, which corresponds to a shade of gray. When the star is being drawn, the brightness value will be used for all three color components in _RGB, from bright white to dark gray.

The brightness *also* affects the speed of the star. The bright white stars are moving fast, while the dark gray ones are moving slowly. This gives the impression of 3D, because things far away move more slowly.

This is called *parallax scrolling* or the *parallax effect*—where things up close move faster than things far away.

Think of mountains while you're riding in the car. Notice how they move *really* slowly compared to signs and buildings on the side of the road. That's what we're copying here by making some stars look far away and some close.

Attack of the Alien Beetles

Now we come to the final finale, the uber example game. I present to you: Attack of the Alien Beetles! Figure 11.7 shows the game running. As you can see, there is a starfield in the background, a bunch of alien beetles, and the player's spaceship (which is shooting!).

Figure 11.7

Attack of the Alien Beetles is a side-scrolling shoot-'em-up game.

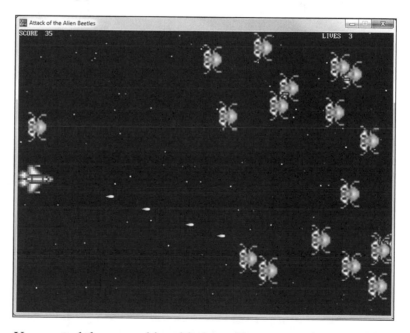

You control the spaceship with the up/down arrow keys, and fire plasma missiles with the Space key. The code for the missiles will be familiar to you because it's the same code we used back in Chapter 9 for Serious Samantha's gun! What has changed is that now the game is drawing an artsy bitmap instead of one made with graphics. The logic is simple: keep shooting the alien beetles until you run out of lives! See Figure 11.8.

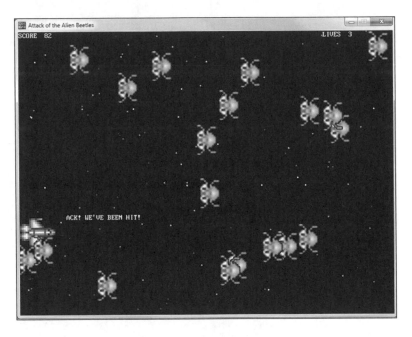

The game requires three bitmap files that must be copied into the QB64 directory (wherever it is installed on your PC—usually C:\QB64).

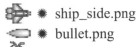

* ship_side.png
* bullet.png
* beetle.png

Now, I'm going to do something completely different in this chapter, something never done before in the history of this *entire* book! I'm just going to show you the entire source code for the game, without any breaks. Not to abandon you to just *figure it out*, but because I want you to study the code. This is the most beautifully written game of the book so far—you can *easily* see how it works by just looking over the code. It's 100% procedural with a sub-procedure for everything!

Early on, nearly every single line was explained in detail. Then we moved along to showing *chunks* of code and explaining each chunk. Then, you should have reached the level where you did not need everything to be explained, so I went over only the new portions of the game in the last two chapters.

Well, now you have reached a level of progress as a game programmer where I think you are capable of seeing the source code for one entire game—without interruption! And also, every single game has been thoroughly reverse-engineered, so it might be refreshing to just see the whole game in one shot.

 SECRET This is a huge game! You might want to load it rather than typing it all in. That way, you can study the program and learn rather than spending so much time typing. But, it's up to you! Typing in the code will help you to learn to be a better programmer, because you're *touching* the code by typing it in, rather than just *reading* it. See the Introduction again for instructions on how to download the files.

Here it comes. Are you ready? Go!

```
'***********************************
_TITLE "Attack of the Alien Beetles"
'***********************************

TYPE Star
    x AS SINGLE
    y AS SINGLE
    brightness AS INTEGER
    speed AS SINGLE
END TYPE

TYPE Sprite
    alive AS INTEGER
    x AS SINGLE
    y AS SINGLE
    width AS INTEGER
    height AS INTEGER
    speed_x AS SINGLE
    speed_y AS SINGLE
    image AS LONG
END TYPE

DIM SHARED scrn&
DIM SHARED lives, score, gameover
DIM SHARED stars(100) AS Star
DIM SHARED ship AS Sprite
DIM SHARED aliens(20) AS Sprite
DIM SHARED bullets(20) AS Sprite
```

```
CALL InitGame
CALL MakeStars
CALL MakeShip
CALL MakeAliens
CALL MakeBullets

'************************
' GAME LOOP
'************************
DO WHILE gameover = 0
    CLS
    CALL DrawStars
    CALL SpriteDraw(ship)
    CALL DrawAliens
    CALL DrawBullets
    CALL PrintInfo
    CALL MoveShip
    CALL CheckCollisions
    CALL GetInput
    _DISPLAY
LOOP
END

'*******************
' InitGame Sub
'*******************
SUB InitGame
scrn& = _NEWIMAGE(800, 600, 32)
SCREEN scrn&
_SCREENMOVE _MIDDLE
lives = 3
score = 0
gameover = 0
END SUB

'*******************
' MakeStars Sub
'*******************
SUB MakeStars
DIM b AS SINGLE
FOR n = 1 TO 100
    stars(n).x = RND * 800
    stars(n).y = RND * 600
    b = 50 + RND * 200
    stars(n).brightness = b
    stars(n).speed = b / 1000.0
NEXT n
END SUB
```

```
'********************
' DrawStars Sub
'********************
SUB DrawStars
FOR n = 1 TO 100
    b = stars(n).brightness
    x = stars(n).x
    y = stars(n).y
    LINE (x - 1, y - 1)-(x + 1, y + 1), _RGB(b, b, b), BF
    stars(n).x = stars(n).x - stars(n).speed
    IF stars(n).x < 0 THEN stars(n).x = 800
NEXT n
END SUB


'********************
' MakeShip Sub
'********************
SUB MakeShip
ship.image = _LOADIMAGE("ship_side.png")
ship.x = 0
ship.y = 280
ship.width = _WIDTH(ship.image)
ship.height = _HEIGHT(ship.image)
END SUB


'********************
' MoveShip Sub
'********************
SUB MoveShip
CALL SpriteMove(ship)
IF ship.y < 0 THEN
    ship.y = 0
ELSEIF ship.y > 520 THEN
    ship.y = 520
END IF
END SUB


'********************
' MakeAliens Sub
'********************
SUB MakeAliens
image& = _LOADIMAGE("beetle.png")
FOR n = 1 TO 20
    aliens(n).image = image&
    aliens(n).x = 800 + RND * 800
    aliens(n).y = RND * 530
    aliens(n).speed_x = -RND / 3
    aliens(n).speed_y = 0
```

```
            aliens(n).width = _WIDTH(image&)
            aliens(n).height = _WIDTH(image&)
NEXT n
END SUB


'********************
' DrawAliens Sub
'********************
SUB DrawAliens
FOR n = 1 TO 20
    CALL SpriteDraw(aliens(n))
    CALL SpriteMove(aliens(n))
    IF aliens(n).x < -64 THEN aliens(n).x = 800
NEXT n
END SUB


'********************
' MakeBullets Sub
'********************
SUB MakeBullets
image& = _LOADIMAGE("bullet.png")
FOR n = 1 TO 20
    bullets(n).image = image&
    bullets(n).alive = 0
    bullets(n).x = 0
    bullets(n).y = 0
    bullets(n).width = _WIDTH(image&)
    bullets(n).height = _HEIGHT(image&)
NEXT n
END SUB


'********************
' DrawBullets Sub
'********************
SUB DrawBullets
FOR n = 1 TO 20
    IF bullets(n).alive = 1 THEN
        CALL SpriteDraw(bullets(n))
        bullets(n).x = bullets(n).x + bullets(n).speed_x
        IF bullets(n).x > 800 THEN bullets(n).alive = 0
    END IF
NEXT n
END SUB


'********************
' FireBullet Sub
'********************
```

```
SUB FireBullet
FOR n = 1 TO 20
    IF bullets(n).alive = 0 THEN
        bullets(n).alive = 1
        bullets(n).speed_x = 1.5
        bullets(n).speed_y = 0
        bullets(n).x = ship.x + ship.width
        bullets(n).y = ship.y + ship.height / 2 - 4
        EXIT FOR
    END IF
NEXT n
END SUB

'********************
' PrintInfo Sub
'********************
SUB PrintInfo
_PRINTMODE _KEEPBACKGROUND
_PRINTSTRING (0, 0), "SCORE " + STR$(score)
_PRINTSTRING (650, 0), "LIVES " + STR$(lives)
END SUB

'********************
' CheckCollisions Sub
'********************
SUB CheckCollisions
'see if ship crashed into any aliens
FOR n = 1 TO 20
    c = SpriteCollision(ship, aliens(n))
    IF c = 1 THEN
        _PRINTSTRING (ship.x + 100, ship.y), "ACK! ↵
WE'VE BEEN HIT!"
        _DISPLAY
        SLEEP
        aliens(n).x = 800 + RND * 400
        lives = lives - 1
        IF lives <= 0 THEN gameover = 1
    END IF
NEXT n

'see if bullets hit any aliens
FOR b = 1 TO 20
    IF bullets(b).alive = 1 THEN
        FOR a = 1 TO 20
            c = SpriteCollision(bullets(b), aliens(a))
            IF c = 1 THEN
                score = score + 1
                bullets(b).alive = 0
```

```
                          aliens(a).x = 800
                    END IF
               NEXT a
          END IF
     NEXT b
     END SUB

     '********************
     ' GetInput Sub
     '********************
     SUB GetInput
     k$ = INKEY$
     IF k$ <> "" THEN
          code = ASC(k$)
          IF code = 0 THEN
               code = ASC(k$, 2)
               IF code = 72 THEN 'Up
                    ship.speed_y = -0.5
               ELSEIF code = 80 THEN 'Down
                    ship.speed_y = 0.5
               ELSE
                    ship.speed_y = 0
               END IF
          ELSEIF code = 32 THEN 'Space
               CALL FireBullet
          ELSEIF code = 27 THEN 'Escape
               gameover = 1
          END IF
     END IF
     END SUB

     '********************
     ' DrawSprite Sub
     '********************
     SUB SpriteDraw (spr AS Sprite)
     _PUTIMAGE (spr.x, spr.y), spr.image
     END SUB

     '********************
     ' MoveSprite Sub
     '********************
     SUB SpriteMove (spr AS Sprite)
     spr.x = spr.x + spr.speed_x
     spr.y = spr.y + spr.speed_y
     END SUB

     '************************
     ' SpriteCollision Function
```

```
'*************************
FUNCTION SpriteCollision (spr1 AS Sprite, spr2 AS Sprite)
SpriteCollision = 0
'test first sprite
cx = spr1.x + spr1.width / 2
cy = spr1.y + spr1.height / 2
IF cx > spr2.x AND cx < spr2.x + spr2.width THEN
    IF cy > spr2.y AND cy < spr2.y + spr2.height THEN
        SpriteCollision = 1
        EXIT FUNCTION
    END IF
END IF
'test second sprite
cx = spr2.x + spr2.width / 2
cy = spr2.y + spr2.height / 2
IF cx > spr1.x AND cx < spr1.x + spr1.width THEN
    IF cy > spr1.y AND cy < spr1.y + spr1.height THEN
        SpriteCollision = 1
        EXIT FUNCTION
    END IF
END IF
END FUNCTION
```

Summary

This chapter went by pretty fast because there were only two new things to learn—moving stars and loading bitmaps. Everything else in this chapter was borrowed from previous chapters. That's one good thing about gaining experience as a game programmer; after a while you get pretty good and start to recycle all of your old code with each new game. This game—Attack of the Alien Beetles— was pretty much just a re-hash of previous game codes. But, where this one really shined, is that we used all of that experience to make it *beautiful* at the same time. When your code looks great like that, you know it will be easy for others to understand it.

Quiz

Here is a little quiz to test whether you were paying attention. Try to answer the questions without looking up the answers first. This is not graded; it will just tell you whether you are ready to go to the next chapter. The answers are found in Appendix A.

1. What command loads a bitmap file as an image?

A. LOAD_IMAGE

B. _LOAD

C. _OPEN

D. _LOADIMAGE

2. Which of the following bitmap file formats is the best one to use for your BASIC games?

A. PNG

B. TIF

C. LBM

D. GIF

3. In order for a bitmap file to be loaded in your BASIC program, where must the file be located?

A. In the QB64 folder (usually C:\QB64).

B. In the Windows folder.

C. In My Documents.

D. In My Pictures.

4. What is the name of our custom type that helps with game objects?

A. Object

B. Graphics

C. Shape

D. Sprite

5. What command draws an image?

A. DRAW

B. _PUTIMAGE

C. DRAW_IMAGE

D. PUT_IMAGE

Homework

Your homework for this chapter is required to prove that you understand what you learned! If you have a hard time with this homework, maybe you went too fast and might need to review the chapter again.

Instructions:

To make the game more challenging, your assignment is to modify the program so that the beetle aliens also move slowly up or down as well as from right to left on the screen. You can use the speed_y property of Sprite to make it work.

Chapter 12

Bomb Catcher

Ⅰn this chapter, you will learn to catch a bomb with a basket. Isn't that usually how it goes when the sky is raining old fuse-type bombs? You grab whatever you can to stop them from hitting the ground? Well, now this situation is no different, and you just happened to have a basket handy. This so-called basket is either a ceramic plant pot or an upside-down autocross racing course cone. But whatever it was previously, now it's a bomb catching basket. This game is surprisingly easy after the last two rather challenging chapters. The really new thing you'll learn to do in this chapter is to play sound effects!

Playing Sounds

To play a sound effect in BASIC, you will need to use an audio file that QB64 supports. Here are the types of audio files that are supported:

* WAV
* OGG
* AIF
* RIF
* VOC
* MID
* MOD
* MP3

SECRET

If you aren't sure where to get audio files for your game, check The Game Creators (www.thegame-creators.com) for an audio collection called "Sound-Matter" with many really neat sound effects.

When you have your audio file copied to C:\QB64 (or the appropriate install folder), then you can load the file using _SNDOPEN.

```
sound_effect& = _SNDOPEN("sound.wav")
```

The next step is to play the sound effect. This is done using _SNDPLAY.

```
_SNDPLAY sound_effect&
```

We will use one sound effect in the Bomb Catcher game coming up in the next section. This is just meant to be an example, not a really exciting game likely to win awards. You can use this great new information to add sound to your own games!

Advanced Keyboard Input

I'm going to introduce you to a more advanced way to get keyboard input. Previously, you have used only INKEY$ to get key presses. That isn't good enough for this game! In order to catch the bombs properly, we need a way to tell the difference between key *pressing* and *releasing*.

To make the game more responsive with keys, we'll use a new command called _KEYHIT. This command returns the key code for a key when pressed *and* released!

```
k = _KEYHIT
```

The pressed code is a positive number, while the released code is a negative number. For instance, the key code for the Left arrow key is 75. When that key is *released*, the code is –75. This is really helpful! To make the code a little easier, it's helpful to just reverse the negative once we know about it, and then treat it like the usual key code again.

To tell whether a key was pressed or released, you can look at whether the code is positive or negative, like this:

```
IF k > 0 THEN 'press
' ... do something
ELSEIF k < 0 THEN 'release
' ... do something
END IF
```

When you want to know if a certain key was released, it's helpful to just reverse the key code like this:

```
k = -k
```

Next, you'll want to examine the special key codes for keys such as the arrows most commonly used in games.

Since the key code comes in as 2 characters (2 bytes), you have to ignore the first part (which is 0), and look only at the second part (the 2nd byte). If you remember, you did this with INKEY$ too, looking at the 2nd byte when that 0 tells you there's a special key code waiting. It's the same with _KEYHIT, but you get the key code a little differently. Instead of copying the 2nd byte, you just divide the code by 256. This causes the code to switch to the 2nd byte, ignoring the first byte.

```
code = k / 256
```

There! So, when you have the code, you can use the same numbers as you did with INKEY$, like 72 for Up, 80 for Down, and so on. Like this:

```
IF code = 75 THEN keyLeft = 1
IF code = 77 THEN keyRight = 1
```

Making the Bomb Catcher Game

Now, I hope you're ready to take on the Bomb Catcher game! There are several places in the program code that deal with sound. See if you can find the code that loads and plays the sound effect! This will play an explosion sound any time you don't catch the bomb!

 For the game in this chapter, you will need to copy the bitmap files basket.png and bomb.png and the sound file explode.wav into C:\QB64 (or wherever you have it installed).

Figure 12.1 shows the game running. It's a pretty simple game, but it is still fun, and it's good to see how games like this work. The best way to learn is to take a simple game and make improvements to it. Can you think of any changes that would make the game more fun?

Figure 12.1

*The Bomb Catcher
game demonstrates
sound effects with
QB64.*

Let's start with the usual suspects we find at the top of most BASIC programs: the title, custom types, variables, and initialization:

```
'***********************************
_TITLE "Bomb Catcher"
'***********************************

TYPE Sprite
    alive AS INTEGER
    x AS SINGLE
    y AS SINGLE
    width AS INTEGER
    height AS INTEGER
    speed_x AS SINGLE
    speed_y AS SINGLE
    image AS LONG
END TYPE

DIM SHARED scrn&
DIM SHARED lives, score, gameover
DIM SHARED background AS Sprite
DIM SHARED basket AS Sprite
DIM SHARED bomb AS Sprite
DIM SHARED keyLeft, keyRight
DIM SHARED explode_sound&
```

```
CALL InitGame
CALL LoadGame
```

Next up in the source code listing is the all-too-familiar game loop! Here we again have a very clean game loop with only calls to other sub-procedures to keep it nice and tidy. That isn't absolutely *necessary* to make a good game, but it helps quite a bit when you want to make changes to the game later. Messy source code is like a messy room: it's hard to find your things!

```
'*************************
' GAME LOOP
'*************************
DO UNTIL gameover = 1
    CALL GetInput
    CALL MoveBasket
    CALL MoveBomb
    CALL CatchBomb
    CALL SpriteDraw(background)
    CALL PrintInfo
    CALL SpriteDraw(bomb)
    CALL SpriteDraw(basket)
    _DISPLAY
LOOP
END
```

Now we come to the InitGame sub-procedure. It's pretty typical now.

```
'*******************
' InitGame Sub
'*******************
SUB InitGame
scrn& = _NEWIMAGE(800, 600, 32)
SCREEN scrn&
_SCREENMOVE _MIDDLE
RANDOMIZE TIMER
score = 0
lives = 3
gameover = 0
END SUB
```

Now for the LoadGame sub-procedure. This is new for this chapter, something you have never seen before! What's so special about it? This cleans up the starting source code (above the game loop) even more! Now instead of calling all of those load- and make- type subs, you just call LoadGame first and then make whatever changes you have to here in LoadGame instead of in the main program. That isn't extremely important, again, but it makes the game easier to read and modify later. This is what programming experts call a standard. It's good to follow a *standard*. That means, something you do every time in your programs.

```
'*******************
' LoadGame Sub
'*******************
SUB LoadGame
CALL MakeBackground
CALL LoadBasket
CALL LoadBomb
explode_sound& = _SNDOPEN("explode.wav")
_DEST scrn&
END SUB
'*******************
' MakeBackground Sub
'*******************
SUB MakeBackground
background.x = 0
background.y = 0
background.width = 800
background.height = 600
background.image = _NEWIMAGE(800, 600, 32)
_DEST background.image
FOR y = 0 TO 599 STEP 4
    c& = _RGB(0, 256 - y / 4, 0)
    LINE (0, y)-(799, y + 4), c&, BF
NEXT y
END SUB


'*******************
' LoadBasket Sub
'*******************
SUB LoadBasket
basket.image = _LOADIMAGE("basket.png")
basket.width = _WIDTH(basket.image)
basket.height = _HEIGHT(basket.image)
basket.x = 350
basket.y = 450
END SUB

'*******************
' LoadBomb Sub
'*******************
SUB LoadBomb
bomb.image = _LOADIMAGE("bomb.png")
bomb.width = _WIDTH(bomb.image)
```

```
bomb.height = _HEIGHT(bomb.image)
bomb.x = RND * (800 - bomb.width)
bomb.y = -200
END SUB
```

Well, that's all for the loading of game assets and making things up with graphics. Now we get to the real core part of the program: drawing, printing, getting user input, and moving sprites. There shouldn't be any surprises here since it's similar to code you've written in previous chapters. The only change is in GetInput, where we are using the new _KEYHIT instead of the old INKEY$.

```
'********************
' PrintInfo Sub
'********************
SUB PrintInfo
_PRINTMODE _KEEPBACKGROUND
COLOR _RGB(0, 0, 0), _RGBA(0, 0, 0, 0)
_PRINTSTRING (0, 0), "SCORE " + STR$(score)
_PRINTSTRING (700, 0), "LIVES " + STR$(lives)
_PRINTSTRING (0, 20), STR$(bomb.width) + "," +
STR$(bomb.height)
END SUB

'********************
' GetInput Sub
'********************
SUB GetInput
k = _KEYHIT
IF k > 0 THEN 'press
    IF k = 27 THEN gameover = 1
    code = k / 256
    IF code = 75 THEN keyLeft = 1
    IF code = 77 THEN keyRight = 1
ELSEIF k < 0 THEN 'release
    k = -k
    code = k / 256
    IF code = 75 THEN keyLeft = 0
    IF code = 77 THEN keyRight = 0
END IF
END SUB

'********************
' MoveBasket Sub
'********************
SUB MoveBasket
IF keyLeft = 1 THEN basket.x = basket.x - 4
IF keyRight = 1 THEN basket.x = basket.x + 4
```

```
IF basket.x < 0 THEN
    basket.x = 0
ELSEIF basket.x > 800 - basket.width THEN
    basket.x = 800 - basket.width
END IF
END SUB

'*******************
' MoveBomb Sub
'*******************
SUB MoveBomb
bomb.y = bomb.y + 2
IF bomb.y > basket.y + 100 THEN
    _SNDPLAY explode_sound&
    lives = lives - 1
    IF lives <= 0 THEN gameover = 1
    bomb.x = RND * (800 - bomb.width)
    bomb.y = -200
END IF
END SUB

'*******************
' CatchBomb Sub
'*******************
SUB CatchBomb
c = SpriteCollision(bomb, basket)
IF c = 1 THEN
    bomb.x = RND * (800 - bomb.width)
    bomb.y = -200
    score = score + 10
END IF
END SUB
```

That's the end of the game logic helper sub-procedures. Now all that remains are two of our old sprite helpers: one sub and one function. The old SpriteMove sub wasn't needed in this program so I left it out.

```
'*******************
' DrawSprite Sub
'*******************
SUB SpriteDraw (spr AS Sprite)
_PUTIMAGE (spr.x, spr.y), spr.image
END SUB

'************************
' SpriteCollision Function
'************************
```

```
FUNCTION SpriteCollision (spr1 AS Sprite, spr2 AS Sprite)
SpriteCollision = 0
'test first sprite
cx = spr1.x + spr1.width / 2
cy = spr1.y + spr1.height / 2
IF cx > spr2.x AND cx < spr2.x + spr2.width THEN
    IF cy > spr2.y AND cy < spr2.y + spr2.height THEN
        SpriteCollision = 1
        EXIT FUNCTION
    END IF
END IF
'test second sprite
cx = spr2.x + spr2.width / 2
cy = spr2.y + spr2.height / 2
IF cx > spr1.x AND cx < spr1.x + spr1.width THEN
    IF cy > spr1.y AND cy < spr1.y + spr1.height THEN
        SpriteCollision = 1
        EXIT FUNCTION
    END IF
END IF
END FUNCTION
```

Summary

That's it, we're done with the chapter, and once again you have shown your skill as a game programmer! So, do you feel pretty good about doing sound effects in BASIC? Loading and playing a sound is pretty easy as long as you remember to copy the sound file to C:\QB64.

Quiz

Here is a little quiz to test whether you were paying attention. Try to answer the questions without looking up the answers first. This is not graded; it will just tell you whether you are ready to move on. The answers are found in Appendix A.

1. What command do you use to load a sound file (like an MP3)?

A. _SNDOPEN

B. _LOAD_SOUND

C. _OPEN_SOUND

D. _FILEOPEN

2. What command do you use to play a sound?

A. _PLAY

B. _PLAY_SOUND

C. _SNDPLAY

D. _RUN

3. What command replaces INKEY$ with more advanced features for key input?

A. _INKEY$

B. _KEYHIT

C. GETKEYS

D. AWESOME_INKEY$

4. In the Bomb Catcher game, what happens if you don't catch a bomb?

A. It blows up!

B. It goes off the screen.

C. It starts over at the top.

D. It starts rolling on the bottom.

5. What is the custom function we created to do sprite collision?

A. FUNCTION Crash

B. FUNCTION Oops

C. FUNCTION Kaboom

D. FUNCTION SpriteCollision

Homework

Your homework for this chapter is required to prove that you understand what you learned! If you have a hard time with this homework, then maybe you went too fast and might need to review the chapter again.

Instructions:

Your homework for this chapter is to—you guessed it!—modify the Bomb Catcher game! Since this is the final chapter, the home-work will be really easy. See if you can make your *own graphics* for the game, and replace the old graphics with your own. That means, making your own bomb picture and basket picture, and replacing the original bomb.png and basket.png with your new drawings. Can you do it? Try opening the files using Paint, or another drawing program, and just change them a little bit, then watch how they look in the game. You could fill the shapes with a different color, for instance!

The End

This is the end of the whole book. If you read every chapter, then congratulations are in order! That's a lot of work, and you should be proud that you got clear to the end!

So what comes next? Do you want to keep learning more and acquire new skills as a game programmer? This book should have given you a good start. There are a lot of other great books that will teach you even more. But for now, how about just working on your own game using the BASIC language and the awesome QB64 compiler?

Have fun!

Appendix A

Quiz Answers

H ere are the answers to the quiz at the end of each chapter.

Chapter 1 Quiz

1. What BASIC command prints out words on the screen?
A. HELLO
[B. PRINT]
C. INTEGER
D. IF

2. What program do we use to write BASIC programs?
A. Visual Basic
B. QBASIC
[C. QB64]
D. BASIC-A

3. Which one of these is a good string variable?
[A. name$ = "Master Chief"]
B. name = 100
C. $name = The Arbiter
D. name$ = Grunt

4. Which one of these is a good number variable?
A. number = "7"
B. number$ = 8
C. number = '4'
[D. number = 5]

5. What BASIC statement lets the program think?
[A. IF...THEN...ELSE]
B. THINK
C. IF...END
D. THINK...STOP

Chapter 2

1. What BASIC statement is used for a remark or comment line (for making notes)?

[A. REM]

B. IF

C. COM

D. NOTE

2. Which command generates a random number (like rolling dice)?

A. INT

B. TIMER

[C. RND]

D. STR$

3. What does RANDOMIZE do?

A. It creates a random number.

[B. It shuffles the random number generator.]

C. It simulates rolling dice.

D. It is like a phaser weapon.

4. What statement starts a loop?

A. DON'T

B. LOOP

C. STAR

[D. DO]

5. What statement ends a loop?

A. DO

B. FOR

[C. LOOP]

D. END

Chapter 3

1. What command creates a graphics window for a program?

[A. SCREEN]

B. GRAPHICS

C. WINDOW

D. CLS

2. What command creates a new image of any size you want?

A. GRAPHICS

[B. _NEWIMAGE]

C. IMAGE

D. NEW_IMAGE

3. What command clears the screen?

A. WIPE

B. CLEAR

[C. CLS]

D. ERASE

4. What command makes colors?

A. CLR

B. COLOR

C. R_G_B

[D. _RGB]

5. Which command gets a key press?

[A. INKEY$]

B. OUTKEY$

C. PINKEY$

D. DINKEY$

Chapter 4

1. Which command gets the time in seconds since midnight?

A. SECONDS

[B. TIMER]

C. GET_TIME

D. TIME_SECONDS

2. Which command gets the current date as a string?

A. CURRENT_DATE

B. DATE

[C. DATE$]

D. GET_DATE$

3. Which command gets the current time as a string?

[A. TIME$]

B. TIME

C. GET_TIME$

D. CURRENT_TIME

4. What statement starts a sub-procedure?

A. SHIP

B. AIRPLANE

C. TORPEDO

[D. SUB]

5. What statement starts a function?

[A. FUNCTION]

B. FUNC

C. FN

D. STATEMENT

Chapter 5

1. Which command gets the state of the mouse?

[A. _MOUSEINPUT]

B. STATE

C. MOUSE

D. EEK

2. What command gets the mouse's X position?

A. MOUSE

[B. _MOUSEX]

C. MOUSE_X

D. MX

3. What command gets the mouse's Y position?

[A. MOUSE_Y]

B. MOUSE

C. _MOUSEY

D. MY

4. What command gets the mouse button state?

A. BUTTON

B. MOUSE_B

C. MOUSE_BUTTON

[D. _MOUSEBUTTON]

5. What statement defines an array variable?

[A. DIM]

B. ARRAY

C. DEF

D. INT

Chapter 6

1. What graphics command draws a line or a box?

[A. LINE]

B. DRAW_LINE

C. _LINE

D. DO_LINE

2. What command makes a new image that's used to draw shapes in the game?

A. IMG

B. IMAGE

[C. _NEWIMAGE]

D. NEW_IMAGE

3. What command draws an image to the screen?

A. DRAW

[B. _PUTIMAGE]

C. DRAW_IMAGE

D. PASTE

4. What command prints words like PRINT, but in graphics mode?

A. FANCY_PRINT

B. DRAW_WORDS

[C. _PRINTSTRING]

D. PRINT_STRING

5. What command draws a circle?

[A. CIRCLE]

B. _CIRCLE

C. DRAW_CIRCLE

D. CIRC

Chapter 7

1. What statement do you use to make your own custom container for variables?

[A. TYPE]

B. CONTAINER

C. BACKPACK

D. LOCKER

2. What type of variable is most often used for numbers?

A. STRING

B. BYTE

[C. INTEGER]

D. DIM

3. What BASIC statement is used for thinking?

[A. IF]

B. DIM

C. DO

D. FOR

4. What type of variable does FUNCTION GetRace$ (n) return?

A. INTEGER

B. DOUBLE

C. LONG

[D. STRING]

5. What statement should you call before using RND to roll random numbers like dice?

A. END

B. CLS

[C. RANDOMIZE]

D. SCREEN

Chapter 8

1. What statement do you use to call a sub-procedure or function?

A. RUN

[B. CALL]

C. DO

D. LOAD

2. How do you declare a global variable that can be used in any sub-procedure or function so that it is visible everywhere in the program?

[A. DIM SHARED]

B. PUBLIC

C. GLOBAL

D. VAR

3. How do you cause the program to pause for 1 second?

A. PAUSE 1

B. REST 1

[C. SLEEP 1]

D. BREAK 1

4. What command causes the screen to be refreshed immediately?

A. _REFRESH

B. _REDRAW

C. _UPDATE

[D. _DISPLAY]

5. What command fills a region of any shape with a solid color?

[A. PAINT]

B. FILL

C. DRAW

D. BUCKET

Chapter 9

1. What BASIC looping statement do we use in this chapter to draw a whole array of Sprites?

[A. FOR...NEXT]

B. DO...LOOP

C. DO...UNTIL

D. DO...WHILE

2. What special technique does the game use to make the zombies seem to walk?

A. Filtering

B. Rotation

[C. Animation]

D. Zooming

3. What is the proper programming term for when two sprites hit each other?

A. Crash

[B. Collision]

C. Bump

D. Smash

4. What command causes graphics output to go to a certain image?

[A. _DEST]

B. _TARGET

C. _IMAGE

D. _OUTPUT

5. How would you declare an array of 50 Sprites called ants?

A. DIM Sprite (AS ants)

B. DIM ants AS Sprite(50)

C. DIM Sprite AS ants(50)

[D. DIM ants(50) AS Sprite]

Chapter 10

1. Which of these is the correct code to define a Sprite variable?

A. Sprite dog

B. VAR dog (Sprite)

C. DIM dog (Sprite)

[D. DIM dog AS Sprite]

2. What command do you use to draw an image?

A. _DRAW

[B. _PUTIMAGE]

C. _PAINT

D. _DRAWIMG

3. Which of the following is the correct way to run a function called MakePaddle?

A. RUN MakePaddle

B. GOTO MakePaddle

[C. CALL MakePaddle]

D. JUMP MakePaddle

4. How do you check for a collision between two sprites?

[A. By checking whether their borders overlap.]

B. By checking the edge of the screen.

C. By checking the width and height of the sprites.

D. By checking the speed of the sprite.

5. What statement do you use to define the data for a game level?

A. LEVEL

B. LOAD

[C. DATA]

D. DEF

Chapter 11

1. What command loads a bitmap file as an image?

A. LOAD_IMAGE

B. _LOAD

C. _OPEN

[D. _LOADIMAGE]

2. Which of the following bitmap file formats is the best one to use for your BASIC games?

[A. PNG]

B. TIF

C. LBM

D. GIF

3. In order for a bitmap file to be loaded in your BASIC program, where must the file be located?

[A. In the QB64 folder (usually C:\QB64).]

B. In the Windows folder.

C. In My Documents.

D. In My Pictures.

4. What is the name of our custom type that helps with game objects?

A. Object

B. Graphics

C. Shape

[D. Sprite]

5. What command draws an image?

A. DRAW

[B. _PUTIMAGE]

C. DRAW_IMAGE

D. PUT_IMAGE

Chapter 12

1. What command do you use to load a sound file (like an MP3)?

[**A. _SNDOPEN**]

B. _LOAD_SOUND

C. _OPEN_SOUND

D. _FILEOPEN

2. What command do you use to play a sound?

A. _PLAY

B. _PLAY_SOUND

[**C. _SNDPLAY**]

D. _RUN

3. What command replaces INKEY$ with more advanced features for key input?

A. _INKEY$

[**B. _KEYHIT**]

C. GETKEYS

D. AWESOME_INKEY$

4. In the Bomb Basket game, what happens if you don't catch a bomb?

[**A. It blows up!**]

B. It goes off the screen.

C. It starts over at the top.

D. It starts rolling on the bottom.

5. What is the custom function we created to do sprite collision?

A. FUNCTION Crash

B. FUNCITON Oops

C. FUNCTION Kaboom

[**D. FUNCTION SpriteCollision**]

Index

Symbols and Numerics

A